LOST
AYRSHIRE
*

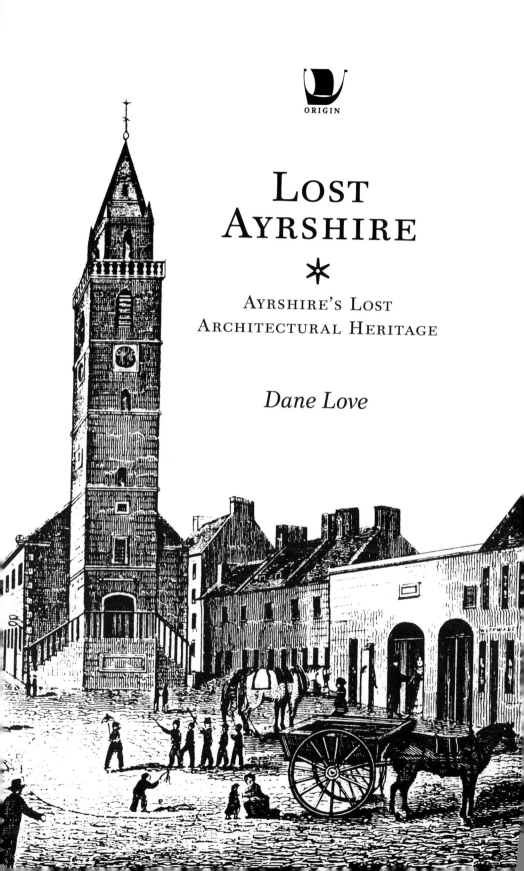

ORIGIN

LOST AYRSHIRE

✳

AYRSHIRE'S LOST ARCHITECTURAL HERITAGE

Dane Love

Previous page:
Irvine Townhead with the old Tolbooth.

✳

This edition first published in 2018 by
Origin, an imprint of Birlinn Limited
West Newington House
10 Newington Road
Edinburgh EH9 1QS

www.birlinn.co.uk

First published by Birlinn Ltd in 2005

ISBN: 978 1 912476 29 9
eBook ISBN: 978 1 78885 1305

British Library Cataloguing-in-Publication Data
A catalogue record for this book is available
from the British Library.

Design: Mark Blackadder

Printed and bound by
Gutenberg Press Limited, Malta

CONTENTS

Kilmarnock Cross.

INTRODUCTION

The ever-changing world in which we live has resulted in mankind's needs and way of life affecting his surroundings. As a result, Ayrshire has lost much of its built heritage, something that must have happened since the beginning of time. One only needs to think of prehistoric remains that are discovered when archaeological digs take place to realise that the buildings of the past have been flattened and built upon for thousands of years, and not just centuries.

This book deals only with buildings that have been demolished or destroyed for which illustrations survive. As a result, it is concerned only with the last couple of hundred years or so, the earliest illustrations of lost buildings dating from the seventeenth century. John Slezer toured Scotland in the 1690s and produced engravings of various views, including some of Ayr and a few other locations. By the nineteenth century illustration and an interest in history had grown, so more drawings and paintings were produced of buildings that were of known antiquity, or else were about to be removed in the many improvements that were taking place. The advent of photography and the popularity of the picture postcard have meant that much of the twentieth century has been recorded on film, although it appears that views of only certain buildings survive, and much has been lost.

It is surprising to find out how quickly some town centres change, something that seems to happen at an alarmingly quick pace. Since the dawn of photography there are many examples of buildings that were captured on the old glass negatives prior to their demolition. The new buildings that were erected in their place have been photographed, and these buildings have in many cases been pulled down in recent years, to be replaced by modern commercial buildings.

Town centres are probably the places where the pace of change is quickest, and successive councils have striven to improve the appearance and prosperity of their burghs. A classic example is Kilmarnock, which seems to have lost more beautiful old buildings than any other town in the west of Scotland.

Admittedly, there were many slums and dangerous buildings in the centre of town, but one only needs to see photographs of Duke Street to see what we have lost.

Kilmarnock's original town centre was built around the ancient Laigh Kirk, its kirkyard, the Old Bridge across the Kilmarnock Water and the burgh tolbooth. Narrow lanes radiated from this central point, and numerous back closes and pends meandered between these lanes, the buildings within them erected in a random fashion. In the early nineteenth century the first major case of modernisation in Ayrshire took place, when new streets were slapped through the centre of town, flattening all buildings in their way. Thus King Street was laid out from the Cross southwards in 1804, a wide thoroughfare that bypassed the ancient and narrow Sandbed Street. New buildings were built along the length of the street, creating one of the finest commercial streets in the county at the time.

Similarly, Portland Street was created, striking northwards from the Cross, in the years that followed the development of King Street. In 1864 the principal road of John Finnie Street was created, the developer being John Finnie, a local coal owner. John Finnie Street is today one of the finest Victorian streets in the county, though there are one or two gaps where modern premises have replaced older buildings, and at the time of writing the former Opera House remains only as a burnt-out façade. The Opera House was erected in 1874 to plans by Kilmarnock architect, James Ingram, but it was destroyed by fire in 1989. The building was demolished, leaving only the sandstone frontage to the main street, preserved for future inclusion in redevelopment. At the time of writing there are proposals for a hotel and commercial building within the site, and hopefully this will come to fruition.

Kilmarnock survived for over 150 years with its new streets, but in the 1960s the town council decided that it wanted to pursue a new phase of modernisation. The architects, Percy Johnson-Marshall & Associates, were commissioned in 1968 to produce a plan for the central area of the town. This was visionary, to say the least, but it really only proposed the wholesale demolition of much of the old town and its replacement with their own idea of what a modern town centre should look like. As a result many old slum properties were removed, as were former industrial premises. At this time a number of old streets were lost altogether, including the noted Duke Street. Fore Street, Regent Street, New Street, Clerk's Lane and Waterloo Street were also to be razed to the ground, to allow the erection of a modern shopping centre. A bypass road was created around this new development, linking West George Street with Sturrock Street. It was this wholesale destruction of

Kilmarnock's town centre that caused the most upset, though no doubt the residents of the early nineteenth century thought the same when what we regard as the fine streetscape of John Finnie Street was erected.

Another major case of town centre redevelopment took place in Irvine. In 1947 Scotland created its first 'New Town', and Irvine was to become the fifth and last one, designated in 1966. Messrs Wilson & Womersley, consultant architects and planners, produced proposals, but these were eventually redrawn. In most other new towns a new town centre on a greenfield site within the designated area was built, leaving the ancient town centre to retire as an example of traditional Scots architecture. However, in Irvine's case the planners decided to use the existing town centre and rebuild much of it. Thus Bridgegate and the centre of the once separate community of Fullarton were flattened, to allow the erection of the modern, if not particularly attractive, concrete blocks of the Rivergate Centre and Bridgegate House. Some areas of traditional building were kept, and even enhanced by restoration work, leaving the centre of Irvine with a mixture of architectural styles, sitting rather uncomfortably together. One only has to walk along Hill Street from the Parish Church towards Bridgegate to find out the difficulty.

Ayr has not been so destructive in its rebuilding. There have been a number of wholesale demolitions, particularly around the Wallacetown district, which was virtually rebuilt in the 1960s and early 1970s, but in the main the ancient street lines survive. Where new buildings have been erected in the High Street they usually stand on the site of older buildings, in line with the street, and being examples of an ever-changing and morphing community. In a number of cases old façades were retained, and new premises erected behind them, such as the BHS building, erected in 1984 to plans by Ian Burke & Partners, but retaining sandstone frontages designed by John Baird II (1816–93), and John Mercer (Ayr Burgh Surveyor), both dating from 1883.

The loss of some of the country's architectural heritage has resulted in council planning departments coming under scrutiny. When Ardmillan Castle, near Girvan, was being partially taken down, with a view to restoration as flats, the council inspectors arrived on scene, and deemed the building to be unsafe. An order for demolition was given, and the building was flattened within a short period in 1990. After the outcry from those who were keen that the building be saved died down, the council admitted that their men were rather hasty in making their decision, and that further guidance should have been sought prior to making the demolition order. Unfortunately, a historic tower house was another victim.

The protection of historic buildings is not something that seems to have advanced much since the Ardmillan case. The Royal Incorporation of Architects in Scotland have produced a wonderful series of books illustrating the best of surviving Scottish architecture. The volume on *Ayrshire and Arran* by Rob Close was published in 1992. A quick glance through the book identifies a series of fine buildings that have succumbed to the demolisher's hammer over the past twelve or thirteen years. Major hospital buildings such as the Kilmarnock Infirmary and Ayr County Hospital have gone. Both were kept for a number of years, hoping that some form of development might take place within the buildings, but the period of neglect had taken its toll and both buildings were eventually taken down. Inns such as the Eglinton Arms in Ardrossan were destroyed by fire, the site now vacant, and the Wheatsheaf Inn in Kilmarnock, one of the oldest surviving inns in the town, found itself isolated within a derelict site, where much of the top of the town was flattened for redevelopment. A fake inn of the same name was rebuilt on the same site, but it is obvious to all but the most disinterested passer by that this is the case, and that the old inn has gone forever. The old corbie-steps on the gable were retained, rebuilt on the new building. Of public buildings the former Lugar Institute has virtually gone, the developer being gradually given permission to remove parts of it until such time as there is nothing worth keeping left, and the Burns Monument in Kilmarnock was demolished in November 2004 following a fire. Domestic houses too have gone. The Walker buildings in Kilmarnock were fine examples of tenement homes, but being located in the midst of former industrial premises, which were no longer working and subsequently demolished, they became ever more under threat. Today a large car park for a trading estate occupies their site.

Developers still try to get rid of old buildings that they find don't fit in with, or hamper their plans. Dunlop House is a fine country house of 1831–4 designed by David Hamilton. For a time a children's home, the building was sold to developers. In 2001 they demolished the old bridge in the grounds, which had been designed by Hamilton and which was Category A-listed. An enforcement order was submitted by the council, which was to make the developer rebuild it as it had been, but they submitted an appeal, resulting in the bridge being rebuilt with a skin of matching stone covering a modern structure.

Other buildings in the county are still under threat. The magnificent Trinity Church in Irvine, built in 1863 to plans by Frederick T. Pilkington, is a wonderfully colourful example of his work, a Gothic feast of decorative stonework, deep lancet windows and large roundel windows. The tall spire is a local landmark, the gablets on it over the windows having coloured stones fanning out like a sunrise over the town. The church has been disused for many years – it served as a community centre but a lack of funds meant that it had to close. With holes in the roof, a new function for it has to be found or it too will find itself listed in any future edition of this work.

Dane Love
Auchinleck, 2005

ACKNOWLEDGEMENTS

In compiling this volume I would like to express my thanks to a number of folk who have allowed me to reproduce illustrations in their collections, or for supplying information. These are: Sheila West and the staff at Carnegie Library, Ayr; Anne Geddes and staff at the Baird Institute Museum, Cumnock; the staff at North Ayrshire Local History Library, Ardrossan; the staff at the Dick Institute, Kilmarnock; the Trustees of Sir John Soane's Museum; Sheena Andrew, and also for pictures taken by her late husband, Ken Andrew; Richard Bain; Frank Beattie; the late James Hunter Blair and others at Blairquhan Castle; Robin Christie of the *Ayrshire Post*; John Clapperton; Patrick Dorman; Nan Cochrane; William Daniel; John Fleming; William Girvan; Betty M. Lees; Stirling T. Mackie of Irvine Royal Academy; and Donald L. Reid.

CHAPTER 1
CASTLES AND TOWERS

ARDMILLAN CASTLE

The old tower of Ardmillan stood on the raised beach to the south of Girvan, tucked into the foot of the wooded hillside. The central core was a U-planned tower house of the late sixteenth century, rising from its vaulted basement through two floors to the attic rooms. The turnpike stairway was located on the inland side of the castle, and climbed up a projecting tower to a square caphouse. On the seaward side of the castle were three huge windows into the Great Hall, and at the corners of the main block were little bartizans. Mary Queen of Scots is supposed to have slept in the castle in 1563.

Writing in 1696, William Abercrummie described Ardmillan as 'so much improven, of late, that it looks like a palace, built round, courtwayes; surrounded with a deep, broad ditch, and strengthened with a moveable bridge at the entry; able to secure the owner from the suddain commotions and assaults of the wild people of this corner, which upon these occasions are set upon robbery and depredation.'

Ardmillan had been extended considerably over its existence, the main addition being the Georgian wing of around 1730, which more than doubled the accommodation. Built at an angle to the original tower, this wing with its central pediment gave the building two different styles, dependent on how one approached it. At a later date, in the 1920s, the Georgian wing was rebuilt in a more haphazard manner to try to blend it better with the ancient tower.

The rebuilding came about as a result of a major fire, something that has dogged Ardmillan over its existence. On 13 October 1919 a fire broke out in the roof and destroyed much of the Georgian wing. Little remained once it was extinguished, and the owner, William Morton, a boot manufacturer based in Birmingham and Newmilns, commenced reconstruction.

Ardmillan was originally one of the Kennedy family's many tower houses, but around 1656 the heiress married James Craufurd of Baidland. He was noted as a persecutor of the Covenanters. In 1855 James Craufurd (1805–76) was appointed a law lord, taking as his title Lord Ardmillan. It was he who inserted

*Top. Ardmillan Castle from the north, showing the original tower
to the right and the Georgian wing in front, prior to its baronialisation.
Above. Blairquhan Castle, sketched prior to its demolition.*

the large windows in the main tower to illuminate 'one of the most spacious and elegant drawing rooms in the country'.

A second major fire occurred in September 1972, requiring seven fire tenders to extinguish the blaze. One lady occupied the castle, and she was killed in the flames. From that time onward the castle quickly went downhill. A caravan site occupied its immediate grounds, and in 1990 the ruins were totally obliterated. Today little more than a baronial gatehouse of 1908 remains to hint at the earlier grandeur.

BLAIRQUHAN CASTLE

The present country house or castle of Blairquhan is a magnificent Tudoresque mansion designed by William Burn (1789–1870). The castle is open to the public during the summer months, and visitors to the house can enjoy looking at the various drawings and schemes for other proposals for replacing the original castle of Blairquhan, which was demolished to allow the present house to be built. Some of the schemes, such as that by James Gillespie Graham (1776–1855), were a remodelling of the original castle, whereas others, like the executed work, were complete replacements of the old tower.

The old Blairquhan can be seen in a sketch of 1787. It depicts a major edifice; a massive castle that would have been a significant monument had it survived. The site of the old castle is now below the manicured gravel in front of the present porte cochere. A few original features do survive, however, and these can be seen in the courtyard adjoining the east end of the present house. Here can be seen some old carved stones, including the original entrance of the sixteenth-century addition, a fine arched doorway with carved border. Over this are the royal arms of King James V. Some of the windows in this courtyard have Romanesque surrounds.

The original tower at Blairquhan is said to have been erected around 1346 by the MacWhirter family, a name that has been spelt MacQuhirter in the past. The Kennedys, who owned virtually everything else in Carrick, acquired Blairquhan through marriage. They erected a large front to the castle, three storeys in height, in 1573. At either end of this block were taller square towers, the corners adorned by bartizans. This major block may have stood separate from the original tower, joined to it only by high courtyard walls.

Blairquhan passed to the Whitefoord family in the early part of the seventeenth century. The Whitefoords were an old Ayrshire family, being chief of their name. However, they invested heavily in the Ayr Bank of Douglas,

Heron & Company and when it crashed spectacularly in 1772 they lost all their investments. The estate had to be sold, and the Trustees of Sir David Hunter Blair Bt purchased it in 1798. By this time the old castle was rather antiquated for his liking and he decided to demolish and build anew, hence the present building, erected between 1821–24.

BLAIRSTON CASTLE

Blairston or Blairstone Castle is one of the many small tower houses that used to abound in Ayrshire, and indeed Scotland, during the sixteenth and seventeenth centuries. Many of them were subsequently demolished as being too damp and cramped for modern tastes, and later houses were usually erected on the site. Many of these tower houses are known to have existed from being mentioned in old charters and other documents, but few illustrations of them are known to survive. The wood-cut depicting Blairston, or Middle Auchindrane as it was also known, was made around 1812. The castle comprised a typical Scots tower-house, though not one of the larger ones. It appears from the sketch to have had only around three floors, but this may be misleading. At eaves level was a single pepperpot turret, built out on corbels. There were neither battlements nor corbels around the roof, indicative of a later period of building. The gables were corbie-stepped. Probably due to the lack of accommodation in the main tower, a lower wing was added alongside, also of two storeys, but the floors were not so high as those in the main tower. William Abercrummie described the building in 1696 as 'a stone tower house with lower buildings about it surrounded with gardens, orchards and parks, it lyes low upon the watersyd'. The castle was the property of Lord Alloway, and shortly after the sketch was made he began extending the tower, the work of which was completed by his son, Elias Cathcart. The house became known as Nether Auchendrane thereafter, and survives as such today one mile to south of Alloway, and four miles from the centre of Ayr.

BUSBIE CASTLE

Busbie Castle was a rather exquisite little tower house that stood on a bank above the Carmel Water, two miles west of Kilmarnock. The tower had three floors, with a fourth located in the attic. The tower at Busbie was probably built in the late sixteenth century by the Mowat family, and comprised a rectangular

Top. Blairston Castle.
Above. Busbie Castle.

plan, measuring 37 feet by 24 feet. The entrance doorway was located on the ground floor, and this led into a small passageway, running in the thickness of the wall. Turning left, one followed the passage into a single room. This had no windows, but on the east and south walls there were wide gunloops. A second ground-floor room was located on the west side of the tower, again with a wide gunloop. In the thickness of the south wall a mural stairway led up to the first floor, which was the tower's great hall. This would have been the master's private stair to his wine cellar, or possibly a route for servants to use between the kitchen, which may have been on the first floor with the great hall, and the ground floor stores.

Busbie had its main stair in the north-west corner of the tower. This was a turnpike stairway, most of which was built into the thickness of the wall. Rising in a clockwise direction it gave access to the first floor, second floor, and to a corbelled-out, square cap-house on the third floor. The second floor comprised two rooms, again a passageway leading from the stair in the thickness of the walls. Each of these rooms had its own fireplace and latrine, the east room also having a mural cupboard, perhaps a charter room.

The roof works of Busbie were rather fine. The attic floor was accessed from the square turret at the stairhead. However, at the other three corners of the attic floor were turrets, circular pepperpot ones in this case. These were adorned with stone string moulds and roofed with solid stone. Together with the fact that some of the principal windows and the entrance doorway were arched made this a rather decorative structure.

The mural corridors and turnpike stair at Busbie were probably responsible for the castle's demise. Even in 1889 when MacGibbon and Ross sketched the tower there was a large crack up the west gable where the spiral stair resulted in thin walls. The tower was abandoned when the replacement Busbie House was erected in the early nineteenth century for H. Ritchie. It stood in a forlorn condition for some time afterwards however, although it looked rather depressed at the fact that its surrounding lands were built on to create the mining community of Knockentiber. The proximity of these houses and the possibility of the tower collapsing led to its demolition in 1952.

CAPRINGTON CASTLE

Although the old tower is incorporated in the present Gothic castle of Caprington which stands by the side of the River Irvine, two miles south-west of Kilmarnock, the style of the original has been so totally lost that it is worth

Caprington Castle as sketched by MacGibbon & Ross, prior to the Gothic additions and alterations.

mentioning in this collection of 'lost' castles. The oldest part of the castle to survive was a late fifteenth-century tower-house, rising through four storeys to an open parapet, built on a corbelled course and complete with open bartisans. It measured around 48 feet by 33 feet. Within this was a garret storey with a heavily-tiled roof. The walls of this tower were 8 feet in thickness and it was erected on a basalt rock outcrop, perched above the River Irvine. The tower had a small stair wing, creating an L-plan building. A later wing was added on the north side of the tower, in which new kitchens and servants' quarters were located on the ground floor. A new doorway was created on the east front. This wing was in the main four storeys in height, but at one point a tower rose to six storeys.

Caprington has been in the ownership of the Cuninghame family for centuries, an ancient charter dated 1385 making reference to them and their castle. Prior to that the Wallaces owned it.

The original tower of Caprington fell into disuse in the eighteenth century, and in 1797 only the ground floor was habitable. The first floor was described as 'unfinished' and the second had no floor. In 1829 Sir William Cuninghame

Top. Corshill Castle from Captain John Abraham Slezer's Theatrum Scotiae.
Above. Culzean Castle as sketched by Robert Adam,
prior to his major rebuilding works.

made plans to rebuild the castle, and encased it in a massive Tudor block designed by Patrick Wilson (*c.* 1798–1871). This incorporated the original tower and spiral stair (converted into a servants' stair). The later wing was demolished, and replaced with a four-storey block. A tall central entrance tower was added, and a new porte cochere erected at ground level to create a new entrance way. The old tower had new windows slapped through the thick walls. Mock battlements and corner turrets were added to retain the castle appearance of what was now a Gothic-revival building. The rock on which the original castle was built was disguised by the creation of false bastion walls.

CORSHILL CASTLE

There actually survives a fragment of Corshill Castle. It stands a lonely sentinel on a low knoll to the north of the ever-encroaching housing estates of Stewarton. Today only a single pillar of masonry and a few barely discernible earthworks survive to mark what was at one time a fairly important seat of the Cuninghame family. In 1789 Francis Grose sketched the ruins, included in his *The Antiquities of Scotland*, and he shows a larger ruined building adjoining the same finger of hoary stone. The engraving shows that the ground floor of the castle was vaulted, indicative of a reasonable age, despite MacGibbon and Ross's claim that it was 'of a late date'. Over the vault there may have been only one floor, with attic above, as the gable of this block survived entire in 1791. Other ruined walls were located around it, creating an L-plan building. Sir David Cuninghame, who abandoned the seat in the second quarter of the eighteenth century, was the last to occupy Corshill. He proposed building himself a new Corshill House near to Kilwinning, but this appears never to have happened. Instead he may have lived at an old house known as Doura Hall, near where the new Corshill was to have been erected. It is known that in June 1845 some repair work was carried out to the ruins in order to stabilise them.

CULZEAN CASTLE

The visitor to the National Trust for Scotland's major property at Culzean sees not an ancient Scottish castle but instead an eighteenth- and nineteenth-century mock castle designed by the famous Robert Adam (1728–92) in what has become known as Adam's castle style. However, prior to this building being started in 1777, admittedly incorporating to some extent part of the original tower, there was an original Scots tower house standing on this imposing headland. The name Culzean, however, does not belong here, for it was transferred to the present location in the seventeenth century. The 'real' Culzean is located two and a half miles to the south, near the present Ballochneil farm. Prior to that the castle at this point was known as Coif Castle, or 'Koif' Castle, as it is depicted on Timothy Pont's map of around 1590. The original castle of Culzean was one of the county's larger tower houses, rising through at least five storeys. The main tower was probably L-shaped in plan, for one of Robert Adam's early sketches of the castle prior to him commencing work depicts the building, complete with a square stair tower in the re-entrant, similar in style to Killochan Castle, near Girvan. Around the tower were lower wings and ancillary buildings, enclosing courtyards and turning their back to the biting winds blowing from the Firth of Clyde. The castle had been rebuilt at 'grate coste and expense' in the 1590s by Sir Thomas Kennedy, and it is probably his rebuilt tower that is shown in Adam's sketches. In 1744 another Sir Thomas Kennedy inherited the estate and in 1762 the title of 9th Earl of Cassillis. He made a number of additions to the castle almost immediately, adding a barrack-like wing of two storeys on the cliff top in the 1760s. Thomas died in 1775 and was succeeded by David Kennedy, and it was he who called in Robert Adam to upgrade the castle. Initially Adam was only to make alterations and improvements to the building, but as the years passed it soon became apparent that David Kennedy was keen to have a showpiece country seat, and entrusted Adam to build the present castle, gradually removing all of the old tower. Today only the walls surrounding the Old Eating Room, or Library, and the Long Drawing or Picture Room survive of the original building, hidden by Adam decoration both internally and externally.

EGLINTON CASTLE

The old Eglinton Castle was an ancient Scottish tower-house to which had been added a 'palace' block, similar to Dean Castle that survives in Kilmarnock. Located north of Irvine, in the parish of Kilwinning, Eglinton was the home of the Montgomerie family, Earls of Eglinton from 1507, but originally the tower was the seat of the Eglintons of that Ilk. The heiress, Elizabeth, daughter of Sir Hugh Eglinton, married John Montgomerie around 1390. The old tower probably dated from the early sixteenth century, for Eglinton Castle was destroyed in a clan battle with the Glencairns in 1527 and was subsequently

The original Eglinton Castle.

rebuilt. It was a rectangular-planned block of four storeys plus attic. The ground floor was vaulted, and a spiral staircase in the north-east corner, partially within the thickness of the walls, wound its way to the parapet. A fine array of stepped corbels, similar to those that survive at Dean Castle palace block or the nearer Stane Castle, projected from the wallheads, and these supported a crenellated parapet. Within the battlements, built on the thick walls, was a corbie-stepped roof, the gables having large chimneys. At an angle to this tower was the palace block, a later, perhaps seventeenth-century, domestic block, built when feuds were less common and domestic comfort more important. This block, which is depicted on a surviving estate plan, was of three storeys, the third-floor windows piercing the eaves and topped with small pediments. Other wings extended from one side of the old tower. In 1729 the great Scots architect, William Adam (1689–1748), was commissioned by the 9th Earl to make alterations to the east side of the tower. He added a new kitchen block and associated back court. Almost half a century later the earls were still not satisfied with their seat and in 1775 commissioned John Baxter Jr

(d. 1798) to rebuild the castle in a grand scheme. This would have produced a rather bland building, but would have kept the old tower. Instead the 12th Earl decided to flatten the building and its wings in 1796 and build a brand new castle, of which more later.

GIFFEN CASTLE

Giffen Castle was an ancient tower located on the edge of a steep bank, between Beith and Dunlop. From its position it commanded a wide tract of countryside, and was the caput of the Barony of Giffen, which formerly extended to one half of the parish of Beith. Originally built sometime in the fourteenth century, the castle was owned by the Eglintons of that Ilk, and then their successors, the Montgomeries. It was gifted to Sir William Montgomerie by his father Sir John Montgomerie of Ardrossan in the middle of the fifteenth century. The castle remained in Montgomerie hands until 1722, when John Montgomerie, MP, Governor of New York, died in debt. Perched on a rounded knoll, which may have been an earlier fortified site, the tower was basically a square structure. It stood 40 feet in height until it collapsed, and a sketch of it drawn in 1835 shows a few windows. Another old sketch shows that it had quite a few openings within the walls, which latterly formed a 'U' shape. Giffen was abandoned shortly after the Montgomeries sold it, and for the next century it acted as a ready quarry for hewn stone. Eventually the last major wall fell down during the night of 12 April 1838. There was no wild storm, and the silence of the night was broken by the thunderous sound of the wall collapsing. Fragments of carved stone from the castle were long to be seen built into the walls of Giffen Mill, which lies a mile from the site of the tower.

HESSILHEAD CASTLE

Hessilhead, or Hazlehead as it is named in some accounts, was an old tower house built in two main stages. It was located in an extensive estate to the east of Beith, in which parish it was located. The older part was located to the east, and at one time was surrounded by large ditches and a loch. The estate was gifted to a younger son of the Montgomerie of Eglinton family. It was here that Alexander Montgomerie (c. 1550–c. 1602), the poet who wrote 'The Cherry and the Slae' in 1597, is said to have been born. He was one of the poets at the court of King James VI. In 1608 the castle was described as 'a strong old building

Top. Giffen Castle as it stood in ruins for many years.
Above. Hessilhead Castle.

environed with lairge ditches, seated on a loch, veil planted and commodiously beautified'. Around 1680 Francis Montgomerie of Giffen acquired the castle from the last Montgomerie of Hessilhead and added a wing to the east, keeping the line of the old tower walls, but as the walls of the newer block were only half as thick, the interior rooms could be larger. On the ground floor was a vaulted kitchen, complete with huge fireplace. An innovative scale and platt stairway was incorporated to supersede the turnpike stairway. Francis Montgomerie also decorated the grounds around the castle, planting avenues of trees in what was regarded as the Dutch style. It was Francis' intention that his heir, John Montgomerie, would occupy Hessilhead. Around 1776 the castle was abandoned and the roof removed. From that time onward the building decayed quickly, the walls crumbling and becoming overgrown with trees until, in the 1960s, the remains were blown up.

LADYLAND CASTLE

The old castle of Ladyland was taken down to allow the erection of the present Ladyland House, which was built sometime between 1816 and 1821 to plans by

Ladyland Castle ruins prior to being cleared away in
order to build the present Ladyland House.

David Hamilton (1768–1843), and which stands on a hillside two miles north of Kilbirnie. The original castle was a typical tower house of the sixteenth century, probably three storeys in height, and was the caput of the Barony of Ladyland. There was a corbelled parapet around the roof, with turrets at the four corners, but this seems to have been altered at a later date, when a more typical pitched roof was added, for W. Hamilton of Ardoch. This was probably executed in 1669, at which time the castle was converted into a more comfortable and less defensive dwelling. The original entrance at first-floor level was opened up and a new pedimented surround affixed to the wall of the tower. The pediment had the date inscribed on it, and the initials W.H. I.B., indicating Hamilton and the Barclay heiress. This pediment was later saved when the tower was demolished and it was incorporated in the entrance gateway to the present walled garden. Other survivals from the time of the castle include a sundial, dated 1673, perhaps commissioned to celebrate the completion of the work in converting the tower. To either side of the main entrance to the castle were low buildings, no doubt stable blocks, but acting rather like wings. When the castle was demolished the men discovered a cavity in one of the walls in which were hidden four small urns, a painted drinking glass and a large jaw bone.

NEWTON CASTLE

Newton Castle in Ayr has been demolished for many years, and today there is nothing to indicate that it ever existed. The site of it is now occupied by a multi-storey car park on the north side of the River Ayr, south of King Street. The multi-storey was not to blame for its removal, for the tower had been removed two centuries earlier.

Newton Castle seems to have been erected sometime in the fifteenth century by the Wallace family, who had previously lived at Smithston, near Mauchline. The tower may have been erected around 1488, when the Wallaces are first styled as 'of Newton'. The tower was described in 1612 as 'a castle and a palace', which may actually refer to two separate parts of the building, similar to Dean Castle, where the old tower would be the castle and an adjoining block would at that time be described as a 'palace' block, referring to its horizontal layout, as opposed to an upright tower building.

Of the layout and content of Newton Castle we can but guess. An old engraving by John Slezer of around 1693 shows it rising to a crenellated parapet, above which was a pitched roof and various chimneys. A second tower may have been built alongside, forming a 'T' or 'L' shape. An inventory

Top. Newton Castle from John Slezer's Theatrum Scotiae.
Above. Ochiltree Castle or House as it was just before demolition.

of 1559 states that the tower had a great hall, kitchen, flesh larder, pantry, ale and wine cellars and five chambers. Many of the rooms were panelled in wood and seem to have been richly decorated and furnished.

On 17 November 1559, at around ten o'clock in the evening, John Wallace of Craigie and forty others forced an entry into the tower and occupied it. At that time the tower was the property of Sir William Hamilton, Provost of Ayr, who had been granted it in 1539 by the king. This, combined with the fact that his estate was ever expanding, caused tensions between the Wallaces and Hamiltons, bubbling into the feud. This seems to have lasted until the 1580s. In 1588 the tower was acquired by the Wallaces of Craigie Castle, after which their ancient seat was allowed to fall into ruins.

Newton Castle suffered some severe damage in a major storm in 1701. The owners abandoned the tower and lived elsewhere until the Georgian mansion of Craigie House was erected on the north bank of the River Ayr in 1730. The tower may have been used by lesser tenants for a time afterwards, but was eventually demolished sometime in the second half of the eighteenth century. Nothing of the tower remains, and the only indication of it in place names is Garden Street, which was built on the site of the walled garden.

OCHILTREE CASTLE

Ochiltree Castle or House stood at the bottom end of the village of Ochiltree, in a garden area bounded by the Lugar Water and what is now the A70 and B7036. The core of the building was an old tower house of the early seventeenth century, but this was extended on a number of occasions to produce a three-storey mansion of sorts, distinguished by its corbie-stepped gables and chimneys. The main block was located on an east–west axis, with a wing extending north at the east end, and a centrally-placed tower containing a stair. The east end of the main block was probably the oldest part of the building, for here was the large chimney flue within thick walls. The ground floor was vaulted, indicative of its age. The walls were six feet thick in places and remained in ruins for many years, for an early account states that large trees were growing within the ruins. At one time the house had dormer windows, but these seem to have been removed, and the carved pediments were for many years left as ornamental features in the gardens. The house seems to have gradually degenerated into a ruin. As early as 1856 it was described as being 'in bad repair and becoming ruinous'. It was abandoned by 1935 and was demolished in 1952, a modern house of the same name now occupying its site. Only the former stable block survives, converted into the present house known as the Coachhouse. Ochiltree was a property of the Colville, Stewart and Cochrane families, and it was probably one of the Stewarts, perhaps Sir James Stewart of Killeth, a son of the Earl of Arran, who built the house. On his death in 1669 the estate passed to the Cochranes, who remained for a century. Later owners were the Cuninghames, who let it in 1785 as a temporary manse. At one time the Boswells of Auchinleck owned it as a dower house to their nearby estate.

PINMORE CASTLE

Pinmore Castle stood at the head of a major meander of the River Stinchar, eleven miles up the wooded valley from its mouth at Ballantrae. At its core was

Pinmore Castle as rebuilt after the first major fire.

a tower house of the sixteenth or seventeenth century, and like virtually all castles in Carrick it was a Kennedy seat. Hugh Hamilton, son of the Rev. Hugh Hamilton of Girvan, acquired it in the eighteenth century. When Hugh died without an heir, the castle passed to his cousin, Col. Alexander West Hamilton, a second son of the Hamiltons of Sundrum Castle. On 22 February 1876, during the ownership of the colonel's son, Hugh Hamilton, the castle was destroyed in a fire. Mr Hamilton was in London at the time, and the castle had been left in charge of the gardener and his wife. Much of the furniture was saved, but the building was gutted. Within a year the ruins were rebuilt and extended in the fashionable neo-baronial style, to plans by Allan Stevenson of Ayr, creating a fairly bulky house. This was in the main three storeys in height, but with an additional attic storey and tall round tower. The castle had the usual corbie-stepped gables and pepperpot turrets, creating an attractive country seat on what has been described by A. H. Millar as 'one of the most lovely bends of the Stinchar'. Unfortunately Pinmore was to suffer a second fire, after which the shell was demolished in May 1982. Nothing of the building remains, and a modern house of smaller proportions occupies the site.

CHAPTER 2
COUNTRY HOUSES

ANNBANK HOUSE

Annbank House stood on the edge of the village of the same name, a few miles east of Ayr. It had a commanding position on a promontory above a bend of the River Ayr, which was dammed at this point in order to drive a mill. Originally the house was known as Privick House (the mill retains this name), but at some point Lady Ann Montgomery married the laird of Privick and Enterkine, and he renamed the house in her honour. In 1788 the house, which was of fairly small dimensions, was repaired and extended for William Cunningham of Enterkine, and no doubt served as a dower house for that estate. The house had little pretension of architectural quality, but was often extended, creating a long block of two storeys. The location of chimneys on the roof hinted at the point where additions were made, and the plans were so random that one end of the house had a gabled roof, whereas the opposite was hipped. By 1884 the coal seams hereabouts were heavily developed, and much of the land west of the house was built on to create Annbank village. The house became the home of the local coalmaster in 1884, this being James Clark. The house was demolished sometime in the 1970s.

ARDEER HOUSE

Ardeer House probably dates from sometime towards the close of the eighteenth century. It occupies the site of an earlier building known as the Ducat-hall, the previous Ardeer House being located elsewhere. Ardeer owed its foundation to the money made from quarrying and mining on the estate. It was anciently a Cuninghame seat, part of the larger Auchenharvie estate, but in 1708 the Rev. Patrick Warner of Irvine (d. 1724) purchased this part of the estate and settled here on his retiral. His daughter married the Rev. Robert Wodrow (1679–1734), who is remembered as the author of *The History of the Sufferings of the Church of Scotland*, and other works. The Warners remained at

Top. Annbank House.
Above. Ardeer House – principal front.

Ardeer for a number of generations, their trustees selling the house to Stevenston Parish Council in 1928 for £5,000. The council sold it on a year later to Nobel's Explosive Company Ltd for the same price, and they converted it into a recreation club for their workers. Ardeer House was a fairly simple block, seven bays long, the central bay projecting on the façade and topped with an unadorned pediment. The exterior corners of the building were rounded. At a later date a porch comprising Ionic pillars was added to the main entrance, over which was a balustraded balcony, reached from the first-floor windows. To the rear was a large addition of two storeys, with a third in the steeply pitched roof, and a large wing with a massive pediment. The house suffered through its life from its proximity to the town of Stevenston, and from the notable sandstone quarry that formerly existed on the estate. The original part of the house was demolished in 1961 and a modern clubhouse erected on the same site, which also was to come down in 1992. Fragments of the original building were retained and survive as a folly.

AUCHANS HOUSE

One should not become confused with the old and new Auchans houses. The old house dates from 1644 and still stands in ruins to the south west of Dundonald, in woodland below the Dundonald Hills. The new Auchans House was built in 1819 or thereabouts, the plans having been exhibited by William Wallace at the Royal Academy. The house, which was a fairly plain block, was built for the Earl of Eglinton, and occupied by his commissioner, originally C. Monteaulieu Burgess and in 1885 the Hon. Greville Richard Vernon, son of the 1st Lord Lyveden. Vernon occupied the house as part of his job as factor to the Eglinton family for many years, though at one time Major Coats of the Paisley thread-making family tenanted it. Five bays in width, the house was two storeys in height. The central bay projected slightly, but at roof level was unadorned by a pediment. In fact, writing in 1885, Millar described its plainness thus, 'No space is lost by the display of architectural eccentricities; and the principal decoration of the main front wall consists of the ivy and other trained shrubs.' On the main front a glazed porch protected the entrance, which led to the hall and main staircase. To the west side was a large conservatory. Some time after Millar had the house photographed in 1885, the main front had a new porch and extended windows added on the ground floor, topped by a balustrade, and it was probably at this time the double-storeyed bay window on the west front was added. There was a considerable wing to the north of the

Auchans House.

main block. Auchans House was sold by the Eglintons to the Earl of Dundonald in 1948, but he did not retain it long before it was demolished in 1970. Its site, with the surrounding parkland, has now been built up with private housing, forming a considerable addition to Dundonald.

AUCHENHARVIE HOUSE

Its site now occupied by Harvey's Leisure Centre, Auchenharvie House was also known as Seabank over its long life. The original house was probably erected around 1708 by Robert Cuninghame as a replacement for the ancient Auchenharvie Castle, which stands in ruins near Torranyard, three and a half miles to the north east of Irvine. In the early years of the nineteenth century Robert Reid Cuninghame (d. 1814) rebuilt the house as his profits from mining grew. He had formed a partnership with the Rev. Patrick Warner of Ardeer as the Stevenston Coal Company. Writing in 1837, the Rev. David Landsborough describes Seabank as 'Sheltered, and sweet, and cheerful . . . with its green

Top. Auchenharvie House.
Above. Bank House, prior to the rebuilding of the wing to the left.

fields, and woody braes, and Martello tower, and mounted battery', the tower a reference to Nelson's Tower that had been erected prior to 1812 when invasion from France was feared. Also demolished, this was a circular tower with splayed base, the upper portion adorned with a corbelled parapet. Robert Cuninghame died in 1868 and the new owners rebuilt the house once more, taking a low baronial appearance, with the addition of corbie-stepped gables and bay windows. The house was probably renamed Auchenharvie at this time. The last owner of the house was James Kirkland, a Saltcoats solicitor. In 1947 the house was sold to the council who converted it into an experimental school for girls. This operated until around 1972, by which time the adjoining Auchenharvie Academy had been erected in the grounds. The school was then closed and the building demolished.

BANK HOUSE

Bank House, which stood south west of New Cumnock, was one of Ayrshire's most difficult mansions to unravel. Few records seem to survive to help date it, but study of the various pictures of it help to piece together the stages of construction. The house probably had an old core of the eighteenth century, perhaps originally little more than a large farmhouse. This is seen to the left in the photograph, which shows the eastern front. At some time in the Victorian period the Italianate wing to the right was added, complete with large tripartite windows, and bays which would have created a very light interior. This block, whose architect is unknown, but which may have been by Robert Alexander Bryden (1841–1906) from the style, was richly finished, with channelled ashlar masonry on the ground floor. The first-floor walls were less refined, simply having projecting quoins, but having a rich corbelled course supporting the eaves. Projecting centrally was a square tower, the ground floor of which had the principal entrance, surrounded with columns. The tower rose to three storeys, the topmost having a viewing room with three arched windows on each front. At a later date the Georgian block on the left had its walls extended upwards, to create a third floor. The level of the original eaves was delineated by a string-course, and the new roofline had a stone balustrade, from which the laird could look out over his lands. An open staircase from the Italianate tower climbed to this platform. The Hyslops acquired Bank and Blackcraig estate in 1781, when a maternal grandfather, William Aird, died. William Hyslop (1854–1936) was the owner of Bank Colliery and founder of New Cumnock Collieries Co. Ltd. The house was demolished in the 1960s.

BELLFIELD HOUSE

Bellfield House was a rather grand Georgian mansion that was gifted by its owners to the people of Kilmarnock and Riccarton parishes, along with its immediate policies. Unfortunately, the authorities seem to have stripped the benefaction to its bare bones, so that today there is little surviving to hint at this great gift of munificence. The mansion was a three-storey block, with additional rooms in the attic, the entrance being by way of steps to the first floor. To the rear the basement floor was above ground level, and on this side there was also a notable bow. The house was probably built in the late eighteenth century. In 1875 Elizabeth, Jane and Margaret, three daughters of Glasgow merchant George Buchanan, gifted the house and 240 acres of grounds to the local communities, along with a fine collection of paintings and over 1,500 books. Known as the Buchanan Bequest, it was proposed that the house would be fitted up as a library and the grounds opened for public recreation. From the funds, sums of money were to be paid to the Ragged School, Kilmarnock Infirmary and the minister of Riccarton, in support of a missionary. The library was to be open to residents of Kilmarnock and Riccarton, and the rest of the house was to be used as an asylum for 'aged and infirm people not on the Poor's Roll, who are 60 years old and upwards, or younger, if rendered unable to provide for themselves by accidental injuries'. However, the collection of books was sold off and the mansion was never used for its intended purpose, being eventually demolished in 1970. The immediate policies were developed as a public park, having a notable rock garden, but this was severely encroached upon by the Bellfield housing estate, and any sense of a former demesne has long since gone.

BRISBANE HOUSE

Brisbane was a rather spectacular old Scots house of 1636, located two miles or so up the Noddsdale or Brisbane Glen from Largs. Anciently there was a house known as Kelsoland here, but James Brisbane of Bishopton acquired the estate in 1671 and changed the name to Brisbane. The house stood rather tall, three storeys in the main, but with three large Flemish gables at the wallheads adding virtually a fourth floor on the south, or main front. The north front had only one of these gables. What it made up for in height, it lacked in width, for the building was only one apartment deep. To the rear was the only staircase in the main block, a single spiral stairway. The gables had crow-steps, and one

Top. Bellfield House.
Above. Brisbane House.

of the skew-putts had the date carved on it. To either side of the main block, added in the eighteenth century when Georgian mansions were all the rage, were two simple pavilions, linked to the old house by quadrants. To the rear a single-storey wing was also added. Probably contemporary with these is the small porch, earlier illustrations depicting the doorway in the main wall. Born here was Sir Thomas MakDougall Brisbane (1773–1860), who became Governor of New South Wales in Australia, and after whom the city of Brisbane and the River Brisbane were named. The house was abandoned in the 1920s, and a plan for restoration in 1938 came to nought. It was demolished in 1942 as a training exercise for Commandos. The old oak front door of Brisbane House was saved and can now be seen in the City Hall in Brisbane, Australia.

CAMBUSDOON HOUSE

Cambusdoon House was erected at Alloway, near Ayr, in 1853 for James Baird (1802–76), one of the richest men in the country at the time. He was the main shareholder in William Baird & Co., ironmasters, which owned many ironworks and mines throughout central Scotland. Cambusdoon was erected the year after his wedding, but his wife survived for just six years. Although he remarried, he was never to be blessed with children. On his death he had an estate worth £1,190,868 14s 5d. He had already gifted £500,000 to the Church of Scotland, and the Baird Trust still gives grants for religious development. The house was a rather grand neo-baronial structure, dominated by its

Cambusdoon House.

impressive six-storey tower, the top of which had a battlemented viewing platform. Adjoining this were the usual wings with bay windows, turrets, corbie-stepped gables, string-courses and panels associated with this period of building. The architect of the house is not known, although it does bear a striking resemblance to work by David Bryce. Bryce's lifework has been studied closely, and no reference to Cambusdoon appears, so it is unlikely that he was responsible. Perhaps a more local architect may have produced the drawings. At some point a new entrance doorway was added, a foursquare block adorned with pepperpot bartizans, and the Baird arms over the doorway. To one side was a large conservatory, and to the other were the service wing, stables and outhouses. From 1926 until 1967 Cambusdoon was used as a private school for boys, but in 1970 it was gutted by fire. The shell of the house remained for a number of years before being demolished. Only a fragment of archway survives to mark the site of the house, its grounds being built upon. Prior to the erection of Cambusdoon, a smaller mansion known as Greenfield stood here, a home of Lord Alloway.

CAMLARG HOUSE

The Craufurds of Camlarg were an old-established family, but they probably owned an earlier tower house that stood on the site of a later Camlarg House, located by the side of the Cummock Burn, north east of Dalmellington. Camlarg was a double-storey building with various additional wings added to

Camlarg House.

it, probably dating from the nineteenth century, though it is unclear if any, or nothing, of the earlier building was incorporated in it. The central block of the house was three bays in length, the doorway located in the central bay. Around the door was a fairly well sculpted arch and pilasters. The masonry comprised coursed stonework, the whole surrounded with smooth banding. The windows had flattened arches and contained Georgian paned glass. To the east of the main block was a single-storey wing, the roof of which was hipped. A similarly roofed extension was located to the west, but in this case was of two storeys. The estate was latterly purchased by the National Coal Board, and occupied by various tenants. A Miss Walker occupied the house until the 1940s, and during the Second World War soldiers camped in the grounds, the officers taking up lodgings in the house. During development of the Pennyvenie Colliery Number 2 the workings came within a short distance of the foundations, rendering the building unsafe. It was demolished in the 1950s. The old entrance gateway to the estate survives at the north end of Dalmellington, and alongside the original drive can be found the Spider Stone, a massive boulder with striations in the shape of a spider's web on it. Other geological specimens that lined the drive have long gone.

CORRAITH HOUSE

Corraith was one of Ayrshire's finest large neo-baronial mansions, built to the plans of David Bryce (1803–1876), the famous Scots architect who was renowned for the style. It stood in open countryside, around one mile west of Symington, and two south of Dundonald, in which parish it was located. The foundation stone was laid in June 1846 by Captain John Deans-Campbell of Correath (sic) and Hoey, and his wife, Margaret C. Hodges, who had a few years previously purchased the farm of Corraith and others adjoining it. A number of coins and newspapers were included in the foundation stone, and these were rediscovered when the building was being demolished. The completed mansion was a fine delectation of corbie-stepped gables and conical turrets. Most, if not all, of the turrets began part of the way up the walls, being corbelled out from square corners. The house had a typically Bryce bayed front, as well as some other features, like the oriel window, which was less like his style. The house was built at great expense, but the stone was obtained on site, so most of the cost was spent on the mason work, and the interior ceilings, which were noted as being one of the main features of the house. Ownership passed to the Mackies of Glenreasdale (near Skipness in Argyll), and thence to

Corraith House.

the Mackie-Campbells of Stonefield Castle, also Argyll. For a number of years the house was occupied by the Scottish Youth Hostel Association, but was closed when Ayr Youth Hostel was opened. The building was eventually demolished early in 1969. One of the leaded windows was saved and is incorporated in the old church at Symington. In the former grounds can still be found the stable block, now converted into a smaller country house, walled gardens, folly and a baronial gateway, the latter erected in 1901.

DALBLAIR HOUSE

Dalblair House was one of a number of large classical houses built on the edge of Ayr by county families. It was built around 1780 in what is Alloway Street, but it had a main doorway to the west, with a long elliptical drive reached from Dalblair Road. The owner was James Gibb, who was the proprietor of a soap manufactory in the town, and also of Dalblair estate in the parish of Auchinleck, which comprised a shooting lodge and grouse moors. The Ayr house was named after the lodge. In the first half of the nineteenth century the house was the property of David Limond, who was Provost of Ayr on three occasions. The architect of the house is not known, but it bears a striking resemblance to other classical mansions in the county, such as Kerelaw, which had similar Venetian windows, or Barskimming, which has the same style of pediment and balustrade along the roofline. Dalblair also had swags under the

31

Top. Dalblair House, prior to the addition of the large porch.
Above. Doonside House.

cornice and below the pedimented piano nobile windows. The attractive pillared and pedimented entrance was later to be covered over by a double-storey extension, three bays by three, which formed a large porch, but detracted considerably from the classical distinction of the original façade. Dalblair House was converted to a hotel in 1895 and it operated as such until 1963. In 1907 the manager of the hotel, Samuel Timbrell, commissioned Allan Stevenson to design a new bar and alterations to the billiards room. In 1924–25 alterations to the hotel were made to the plans of James Miller. The house and lands were purchased for development, the hotel being flattened and Dalblair Shopping Arcade (now Arran Mall) being erected on the site.

DOONSIDE HOUSE

The great Victorian pile of Doonside, which stood on the south side of the Auld Brig o' Doon at Alloway, was erected sometime around 1889, to plans drawn up by J. MacVicar Anderson (1835–1915). Anderson was the nephew and successor to William Burn (1789–1870), a noted Scots architect who produced many fine country houses, often in the Tudor, Jacobean or Elizabethan style. Anderson himself was responsible for many other country houses, but few in Scotland, which makes Doonside's loss all the more sad. He was also an accomplished landscape painter. Various plans by Anderson for the house survive, dating from 1884 to 1889, and the house was no doubt built at this time. A bulky Jacobean structure, Doonside was distinguished by its four-storey tower, capped with an ogival lead roof. At first-floor level was a lengthy balcony, stretching the length of the garden front, and reached from an external stairway, as well as from the doorways from the main rooms. Inside, the main rooms were arranged alongside a spinal corridor. A secondary wing, used by the family when not entertaining, was located to one side, and this overlooked part of the garden. Doonside was built for William Hamilton Dunlop, a solicitor and bank agent in Ayr. It was he who was influential in transferring ownership of Burns's Cottage from the Shoemakers' Incorporation of Ayr to the Trustees of the Burns Monument. He was also the proprietor of the *Ayr Advertiser*. Doonside replaced an older Georgian building that was damaged by fire around 1880. It had been a Crawford property. The Jacobean house was itself demolished in 1961 for being too large. Much of the original panelling was preserved and installed in the former home farm, creating a new Doonside House. Many of the balusters were also preserved, and these form divisions in the gardens.

THE LATTER
EGLINTON CASTLE

The latter Eglinton Castle was a massive Gothic castellated mansion, erected in 1796–1812 by Hugh Montgomerie, 12th Earl of Eglinton (1740–1819), on the site of the original castle. The old tower was removed and a huge building erected in its place. The architect was John Paterson (d. 1832), whom Robert Adam originally employed prior to his death. Unfortunately, Paterson did not have Adam's flair for originality and instead produced a building that relied more on its bulk for impressing than its style. The main block had a four-square appearance, with tall round towers at the corners. These were five storeys in height, the first and second being considerably higher than the rest. The main façade between these towers was nine bays in length, the central five being advanced and slightly bayed in the centre. Most windows, which were rectangular, were adorned with hoodmoulds, and a stringcourse separated the second and third floors. The crenellated parapet was supported on a corbel course, and the projecting bay had pepperpot turrets at the corners. Right in the middle of this main block rose an ever taller tower, octagonal in plan, with a flat roof from which an extensive view could be had of the policies. This tower contained the saloon, which measured 36 feet in diameter and which was open to the top. The main apartment measured 52 feet long, 32 feet wide and 24 feet

The latter Eglinton Castle.

in height. Attached to the main block were extensive wings, some considerable buildings themselves, with up to three floors. The main entrance to the castle was made through a large porch. Sometime between 1857 and 1860 there were a few alterations, mostly of a castellated style, made to plans by William Railton of Kilmarnock. The Eglintons lost money in a variety of schemes, the most famous being the Eglinton Tournament of August 1839, which cost the 13th Earl around £40,000, but this was only the most public of their spending. The castle became too large to maintain, and in December 1925 the family vacated it. Soon after this the roof was removed, and the ruins became a target for shell practice by the Royal Engineers. In the 1970s the grounds were acquired by the Clement Wilson Foundation and made into a public park. Most of the ruins were cleared away in 1973, leaving only one of the corner towers of the main block standing, and a double-storey façade of the west wing. Other foundations survive to mark the shape and extent of the original building.

ENTERKINE HOUSE

The present Enterkine House, which operates as a high-class hotel and restaurant, dates from 1939 and was designed by John Fairweather & Sons of Glasgow. It stands on the site of an older building, which is thought to have

Enterkine House.

35

been erected in the late eighteenth century for the Cunninghame family, a branch of the Cunninghames of Caprington Castle, who long owned the estate. In turn, the Georgian house had been erected on the site of an older castle or tower house. The house comprised a main block four storeys in height, the entrance being located at first-floor level, the basement being sunken at this side. The principal façade comprised five bays, the middle three projecting beyond the rest. A large porch with arched openings was probably a later addition. Severely Georgian in style, the main façade was enlivened with the addition of Venetian windows at first-floor level, lighting the principal apartments within. The roof was hipped, and there were two large banks of chimneys on it, similar in style to a number of other Ayrshire mansions. Enterkine was owned by a number of families, historically being associated with the Dunbars, but being passed to a branch of the Cuninghames. At the time of Robert Burns the house was owned by William Cunninghame, who was responsible for organising the 'Fête Champêtre' referred to in one of the bard's songs. This took place on the holm below the house, and was supposed to have been organised by Cunninghame to try to influence the local nobility to elect him as MP for Ayrshire. In 1830 John Bell, a notable figure in the political life of the county, acquired the estate.

FINNARTS HOUSE

Finnarts (or Finnart, as it was also known) was one of those grand old Scots lairds' houses whose loss is much to be regretted. Country houses of this scale are more manageable than the huge rambling architect-designed mansions of the eighteenth and nineteenth century, and had it survived for much longer it would have formed an ideal restoration prospect. Finnarts stood in the lower part of Glen App, at the foot of the Altygunnach Glen, and was thus probably the southernmost country house in the county. The main block was a typical laird's house, perhaps of the seventeenth century, to which various wings had been added and alterations made during its life. The main entrance was through a small porch, the gable of which formed an armorial pediment, topped with a carved rendition of the owner's crest. The block to the right of this was probably a later addition, as was the western wing, which had a dominant single-storey round turret facing the courtyard. The estate was anciently part of the Kennedy lands, but in 1930 C.F. Kennedy sold the house and 4,000 acres of land to Lord Inchcape, owner of Glenapp Castle. After this the house was no longer the main residence on the estate, and it was subsequently demolished.

Finnarts House.

Little survives of what was an ancient estate, other than a cylindrical doocot on the hillside above.

FULLARTON HOUSE

The loss of Fullarton House, on the outskirts of Troon, is one of the greatest tragedies of Ayrshire's lost architectural heritage. The mansion was one of the finest Robert Adam buildings in the county, although the main central block, which was seven bays wide, and rising through three storeys to the attic floor, was erected earlier and by an unknown hand. William Fullarton had the central block erected in 1745, a fine classical block, the central three bays on both fronts projecting slightly, and a number of windows adorned with arches and 'portholes'. Internally there was a rather grand staircase, and a secondary spiral stair for the servants. In 1790 Col. William Fullarton of that Ilk proposed replacing the house with a new castle-style mansion, but the plans for this were cut back considerably, and only the new stable block was erected in Robert

Top. Fullarton House.
Above. Girgenti House.

Adam's inimitable style. The main house had extensions added at this time, some of which sported crenellations to hint at a castle, but which failed to change the overall appearance of what was still basically a Georgian mansion. Fullarton died in 1808, the last of an ancient family that had held Fullarton estate since the thirteenth century, and the estate was sold to the Duke of Portland. He had no real need for the mansion, but bought it to allow him to develop his Kilmarnock estates by allowing the creation of a railway to the new harbour at Troon that he was developing. Although he stayed in the house for a time, it was mainly let out. The last occupier of the house was Lord Glenarthur, who leased it for 40 years. In 1928 the house was purchased by Troon Town Council. Unable to let it complete, in 1930 they divided it into four dwellings. The house became troublesome due to rot, and in 1966 it was demolished. The stable block and some other structures remain; the former was converted into smaller homes in 1974.

GIRGENTI HOUSE

Girgenti was a rather strange-looking country house, described by John Shedden Dobie in 1876 as having a 'somewhat fantastic order of architecture' and by the writer of the *New Statistical Account* for the parish of Stewarton as being in 'rather an uncommon style'. Captain John Cheape acquired the lands of Bonnyton from Tomas Reid of Stacklawhill in 1827, shortly after retiring from the army. Captain Cheape was descended from Fife stock, being a son of the Cheapes of Sauchie in Clackmannanshire. After changing the name of Bonnyton to Girgenti, he set about erecting a rather eclectic home for himself. Prior to this the lands were rather barren, but Cheape spent the rest of his life planting and improving the estate. The house was not overly big, being basically single storey in appearance, but was adorned with over-large architectural features for the size of building. These included the pillared portico, dormer windows on two levels and capped tower. To one side was a large extension with a bayed projection and a sizeable summer house. Captain Cheape died unmarried in 1850 and the estate was sold to allow funds to be given to various infirmaries across Scotland. It was bought by William Broom, an iron master from Glasgow, but later passed to Alexander Cochrane of Verreville in Lanarkshire. The house was demolished in the 1940s, leaving a few remnants of Cheape's buildings. These include two Italianate gate lodges and a tall octagonal bell-tower, complete with clock and louvred openings. The old walled garden also survives.

Top. Glenbuck House.
Above. Highthorn House.

GLENBUCK HOUSE

Glenbuck House stood at the eastern extremity of Ayrshire, where the main Ayr to Edinburgh road leaves the county. Built for Charles Howatson in 1879, the house was a fine baronial structure designed by John Murdoch (1825–1907) of Ayr. Murdoch was a fairly prolific architect in the county, but started his career as a civil engineer, which may have influenced some of his designs. He became an architect in 1850. He was responsible for a number of churches in the county, some of which still survive, such as the large St Leonard's Church in Ayr, and the smaller Cumnock Congregational Church, as well as numerous public buildings and schools. Of its style, Glenbuck was one of the more successful imitations of a Scottish tower house, for it was generally taller than it was wide, and it had a dominant round tower in the re-entrant, at the foot of which was the main entrance. On the external corner of the house was a secondary turret, corbelled out from first-floor level and topped with a tall conical roof. Charles Howatson (1833–1918) was a self-made man who came to prominence when one of his blackface rams won the Prince of Wales Gold Medal at the Royal Highland Show. His estate extended over much of the moorland around Muirkirk, from the Glenmuir valley north to the Lanarkshire boundary. Howatson was the main landowner in the district, and he was responsible for erecting Glenbuck Church, now demolished, and the Covenanting martyrs' monument in Muirkirk. Glenbuck House was demolished in June 1948.

HIGHTHORN HOUSE

Highthorn House was also known as Highthorn Castle, a rather grand name for a fairly plain house to which baronial additions had been made. The house was located off Meadowfoot Road in West Kilbride, and was erected for Mrs Boyd, the mother of General Sir Archibald Hunter (1856–1936). The site of the house was originally an old smithy, complete with joiner's workshop, but a typical Georgian country house of average size replaced these sometime in the nineteenth century. This was two storeys in height, and was noted for its large bay windows, rising through two floors, and forming the dominant architectural feature. This original house can be seen creating the central portion of the building in the photograph. Late in the nineteenth century the house was more than doubled in size, with the addition of two wings to either side of the old house. These were built in the neo-baronial style that was then in vogue, with high corbie-stepped gables and turret roofs. The new wings were more prominent than the central block, making the house seem rather disjointed. Unlike many other extensions added to country houses, where the style of architecture was changed, there was little attempt to disguise the old block and try to make it match the new style. The only attempt at this here was the addition of a small corbie-stepped gablet over the central window above the main entrance door. Highthorn was demolished sometime before the Second World War.

HOLMES HOUSE

Holmes (or Holms as it appears to have been spelt in the past) was one of a group of rather fine Tudor mansions that sprang up in Ayrshire in the early nineteenth century. More ornamental than some, Holmes had the usual selection of corner-towers, hoodmoulded windows, porte cochere, crenellated battlements and Gothic traceried windows, but was noted for its small bell-tower and corner turret. The masonry work was rather fine, all the stones accurately chiselled and tight-fitting. On the east front, one of the windows incorporated an ecclesiastical window, with three ornate lancets, hinting that inside there may have been a chapel. The architect of the house is not known, but it has been speculated that it could have been David Hamilton, William Burn, Thomas Hamilton or William Wilkins. The house was probably built for Lieut.-Col. James Fairlie of Bellfield, who succeeded to the estate in 1819, or Mungo Fairlie, who had made his fortune in the East and West Indian trades and bought the estate in 1796. A later James Fairlie died in 1926, leaving £25,288 in his will. The Fairlies were cadets of the Fairlies of that Ilk. The house sat in a small estate, but in 1935 it was apparently abandoned. With damp and rot running rife throughout the mansion, the building was sold soon after and stripped of its internal furnishings and roof. The main structure was demolished, leaving only a few overgrown fragments standing. Some of the home farm buildings survive, as well as a rebuilt gatehouse.

KAMESHILL HOUSE

With the arrival of the ironworks and associated industries in Muirkirk, a number of larger country houses were erected as homes for the managers. Thus

Top. Holmes House.
Above. Kameshill House.

Kameshill, which stood on the south side of the River Ayr at Muirkirk, was acquired and rebuilt for the manager of the local collieries. Kameshill was originally a large farmhouse known as High Hill, but in 1790 it was rebuilt considerably for Joseph Hutchison. A new mansion was erected using local sandstone, the bulk of the building being of two storeys, although one part was taller, having a third storey partially within the roofspace. There was little to distinguish Kameshill architecturally, other than the large string course that made its way around the building approximately at first-floor level. The main entrance was located within a re-entrant angle on the main front, where a number of gables faced onto the drive. The architect of the building is unknown, but the house did have a similarity to Wellwood House, which stood nearby, in its use of string course and paired windows. Where Wellwood had corbie-stepped gables and was more baronial in appearance, Kameshill had flat skewstones supported by skew putts. Kameshill House was demolished in 1956.

KERELAW HOUSE

Kerelaw House was a tall block comprising three storeys plus an attic, located on an elevated site above the town of Stevenston. It was built in the grounds of the ancient Kerelaw Castle, the ruins of which survive. Alexander Hamilton probably built the original house in 1778. The mansion had a classical Adam look about it, the entrance front having five bays, the central one of which was projecting and was topped by an unadorned pediment. The house was three bays in width but never had any wings, making it look rather tall and isolated. The walls had rusticated quoins, but the main ornament to the principal front was the pillared portico, which supported a balcony reached from a Venetian window at first floor level. This window was included within a white arch. Kerelaw later became the property of the Fullartons, who owned plantations in the West Indies and who adorned the policies with a variety of exotic plants. James Campbell purchased the house in 1919. His youngest son, Kenneth Campbell, became a pilot with the RAF Volunteer Reserve, but lost his life at the age of 24 whilst attacking the German battleship *Gneisenau* on 6 April 1941. He was awarded the Victoria Cross posthumously on 10 March 1942. The house itself was demolished shortly after 1970, having been bought by Glasgow Corporation in 1963 to become part of a List D school (replacing Mossbank Approved School at Millerston). The school was designed to accommodate 80–90 boys aged 13–14.

Kerelaw House.

LAGGAN HOUSE

Laggan House, which stood at the foot of Glen Tig, near to the confluence of the Water of Tig with the River Stinchar, two miles from Ballantrae, was a large 'High' Victorian mansion, perched on a bluff overlooking the Tig. The architect of the building is unknown, but it has tantalisingly been associated with David MacGibbon (1831–1902), the architect and famous co-author with Thomas Ross of *The Castellated and Domestic Architecture of Scotland*, published in five volumes between 1887 and 1892, as well as the three-volume *Ecclesiastical Architecture of Scotland*, which followed in 1896–97. After having studied virtually every major castle in Scotland, it is hoped that he learned more from them than to create what has been described as a Victorian monstrosity, with no acknowledgment to the baronial style of the past. Perhaps MacGibbon had nothing to do with Laggan, for it was his father, Charles, who bought the estate of Laggan and Garleffin in 1845 from the Earl of Stair. He was a building contractor who was responsible for building much of Edinburgh's New Town and numerous country houses across Scotland. Nevertheless, Laggan is similar in style and finish to Cormiston Towers, which stood near Biggar in

Lanarkshire, and which is known to have been David's work, and Laggan was gifted to him in life-rent by his father in 1865. Similarly, Ashfield, his Edinburgh house erected in 1874–75 to his own plans (it is also demolished), was a Victorian baronial structure which later tastes dismissed as unauthentic. The house erected at Laggan adopted the Victorian's version of what a Scottish castle should be like, with tall candle-snuffer turret roofs, crenellated parapets, corbie-stepped gables and string courses. The walls were built of coursed rubble, with wrought quoins and surrounds to the windows. David MacGibbon died in 1902 and a bronze memorial in Ballantrae church commemorates him. In 1913 a new wing was added to Laggan House, designed by James Miller of Ayr (1860–1947), who adopted the old Scots style developed by Sir Robert Lorimer. The house was demolished for the most part in the 1940s, leaving only the billiard room and the 1913 wing standing. The billiard room, which was retained as a shell, stands apart from the Miller wing, which is a considerable house in its own right, but which would benefit from the reinstatement of the turret roof.

LOGAN HOUSE

Logan House was one of those attractive small mansions that were erected all over Scotland, usually at the end of the eighteenth or early in the nineteenth centuries, where the architect remains obscure. Logan was probably erected for Hugh Logan of that Ilk (1739–1802), a notable wit in his day, and a contemporary of Robert Burns. Logan lost heavily in the Ayr Bank Crash of 1772, but seems to have held on to some of his estate until his death. Hugh was the youngest of three sons, and when his father asked him what he'd like to do for a living, he replied, 'I'll just be a laird, like yourself.' His elder brothers did die before his father and Hugh inherited at the age of 21. According to an early historian of Ayrshire, James Paterson, Logan's 'racy humour was wont to keep the festive table in a roar, and whose extreme hospitality is still spoken of with feelings of palliative respect.' The writer of the *New Statistical Account* frowned on Logan's 'coarseness and profanity', which no doubt was enjoyed by Robert Burns, who refers to 'Squire Hugh' in one of his mock epitaphs. A book of humour entitled *The Laird of Logan* was published in the nineteenth century and went through many editions. Logan House was three storeys in height, the main rooms located on the piano nobile, reached by a sizeable fore stair which led to the bayed centre of the main front. On the south side of the house was a large conservatory and glasshouse, the conservatory perched at first floor level,

Top. Laggan House from the gardens.
Above. Logan House.

and added in the second half of the nineteenth century. The house remained in Logan hands until 1798, when it was sold to a Mr Hamilton from Glasgow, who sold it on to William Allason. By the time of the Second World War the house was more or less abandoned, being only partially habitable, and the estate was put up for sale. Purchased by Ayr County Council in 1948, the lands were developed as a small housing scheme, in order to rehouse families from the miners' rows at Lugar and Cronberry. The house survived for a short time within the estate until it was demolished in 1949. Nothing of the former stable block or gatehouse survives, only the street name Logan Avenue with a few stumps of trees indicating where the main approach was at one time made. It is claimed that a summer house from the estate survives in Dunbartonshire, and that the sundial was moved to Perthshire.

MANSFIELD HOUSE

Mansfield was not one of the most endearing of country houses, but it was an attractive one nevertheless. It was located one and a half miles east of New Cumnock, on the north side of the River Nith. Erected some time prior to 1857, the house was probably an amalgam of various building periods. Mansfield House was the home of the Stuart-Menteth family, who became Baronets of Mansfield and Closeburn Castle in Dumfriesshire in 1838. Sir

Mansfield House.

Charles, 1st Baronet (1769–1847), patented a three-draw kiln for the manufacture of lime, used as a fertiliser and for mortar, and from this added to his
fortune. A number of old limeworkings still survive on the former estate. Sir
Charles also developed the coalfields on his estate, and greatly improved the
condition of the fields on his farms. The entrance front of Mansfield presented
three main gables to the drive, a fourth incorporated in the porch, which was
adorned with the Menteth arms in a lozenge – a *bend chequy* and three buckles.
This porch was quite unique in that it was glazed on the walls and roof. The
building was Italianate in style, with decorative fascias. On two fronts the
house had large bay windows, extending through two floors. Sir William F.
Stuart-Menteth, 5th Baronet (1874–1952), put the house and estate on the market
in 1937, at which time the estate extended to 2,300 acres. The house was
demolished in 1957. Little remains to indicate that there was once a considerable country house here, other than a few walls that are too large and well-
made for the farm that remains, and a former gatehouse.

MONTGOMERIE CASTLE

Also known as Coilsfield when it was first built in 1804, Montgomerie was one
of the finest mansion houses in Ayrshire. It stood on rising ground above the
Water of Fail, south east of Tarbolton. The house was built for Colonel Hugh

Montgomerie Castle.

49

Montgomerie (1739–1819), who became the 12th Earl of Eglinton in 1796 on the death of his kinsman. The house was built to plans drawn up by John Paterson, Robert Adam's successor. An earlier castle stood on the site, referred to by Robert Burns in his works, for here his love, Highland Mary, worked in the byre. The house contained a number of circular and bayed rooms, in a style similar to Adam's, with a large round vestibule at the entrance. To either side of this were the drawing room and dining room, the former having curved ends. Beyond was the main pillared hall, off which were two staircases, and beyond was the bow-fronted library. Externally the house was distinguished by its pillared bow front, the top of which was adorned by a lead dome. Paired pilasters marked the end of the main block, which had two main floors over a basement and an attic above, the light-coloured stone contrasting with the darker stone infill. To either side were lower wings, the southerly occupied by a conservatory and plant room, the northerly by the butler's pantry and staff accommodation. The Eglinton family sold Montgomerie to the Patersons, R.P. Paterson owning 2,552 acres around it in the late nineteenth century. Montgomerie became a country house hotel after the Second World War, but trade declined and the owners could not keep up with the maintenance costs. They left the building in March 1969 and within a month the building was destroyed by fire. The shell remained for a time before it was eventually demolished, as were the former game larder, stable block, gatehouse and ornamental bridge. Today the policies of Montgomerie have been shorn of much of their woodland, the parklands returned to agricultural fields and a caravan site occupies the former gardens.

NETHERPLACE HOUSE

Netherplace House stood on the edge of Mauchline and was an ancient mansion to which an attractive Tudoresque frontage, adorned with octagonal corner turrets and unique Jacobean wallheads, was added. The original house, which probably dated from 1620, was somewhat hidden to the rear, but it was a rather fine Scots Georgian building, rising through three storeys. Old accounts name the building Cowfauldshaw. This was built for Mungo Campbell, a scion of the Campbells of Loudoun. The Tudor block was erected after 4 April 1827, when the foundation stone was laid, though the architect is unknown. This was only two storeys in height, but they were much taller storeys, and resulted in a block of a similar height to the three-storey original block. To one side was a lower wing, also of two storeys. Minor alterations

Netherplace House: the Tudor wing.

were undertaken in 1901–02 to plans by Allan Stevenson of Ayr. The main entrance was located behind a large Gothic porch. Each Georgian window had heavy hoodmoulds. Netherplace was so named as it was the lower of the two 'places' of Mauchline, and it was for many years the seat of the Campbell, then Hamilton-Campbell family. At one time Robert Burns had a disagreement with Lilias Campbell, and in revenge composed verses in which he refers to her as 'Queen Netherplace'. For many years the house was leased out, and among tenants were Lord Justice Clerk Hope. His son, Lieutenant Hope, won the V.C. for his acts of gallantry at Sebastopol. On his return home there was a large fireworks display in the grounds. Other tenants included Mrs Middleton, the widow of a tea-planter, whose son was an equerry to Elizabeth, Empress of Austria, and James Baird Thorneycroft, director of James Baird & Co., ironmasters. The last main owner of the house was Colonel Mungo Hamilton-Campbell, who died in 1951. After his death the house, which had developed dry-rot, was abandoned then demolished, and the estate was broken up in 1954. Most of the immediate policies have been built on with private dwellings, but two former gate lodges survive. Lost with the demise of the grounds was an ancient yew tree, claimed to be over 700 years of age, and which had grown to over thirty feet in height and with a circumference of fifty yards. The canopy of 'The Big Tree' formed an umbrella under which children would play for hours.

Top. Newfield House.
Above. Orangefield House with its airport control tower perched on the roof.

NEWFIELD HOUSE

Newfield was a rather strange-looking building, almost a collection of architectural styles assembled into one house. It stood to the east of Dundonald, on an elevated location overlooking the valley of the River Irvine. The original house may have dated from around 1725, when Captain Nugent owned the estate, but the house as it latterly existed was probably a nineteenth-century collection of additions. Captain Nugent had been active at the Battle of Nieufeldt in Germany and is said to have renamed the old estate of Galrigs after his victory. A nearby farm retains the name Galrigside. The entrance front of the house comprised two corbie-stepped gables with a central connecting block, from which projected a heavy porch, adorned with arms. This would have been a fairly plain front, but over the first floor windows were rather large carvings inset above the lintels, and roundels were placed on the gables. To one side was a large double-storey bay window, the roof of which was domed and contained a dormer window. To the other side was a tall tower, topped with a French-style roof with iron railings around what was no doubt a tiny viewing platform, reached from a trapdoor. A lower wing was located to the side of this tower. Later owners included Colonel Crawford, who owned the estate in the mid nineteenth century, the Finnie family of coalmasters and Sir Charles MacAndrew. MacAndrew was MP for Kilmarnock Burghs and Deputy Speaker of the House of Commons. Newfield House was demolished in 1964.

ORANGEFIELD HOUSE

The house of Orangefield had a strange history. An older house, which was known as Monkton House, stood on the site, but around 1736 the estate was acquired by James MacRae (1677–1748). He had emigrated to India where he was a successful merchant and was active in politics, becoming Governor of Madras. When he retired he had amassed a large fortune, which he brought back to Scotland. Rebuilding Monkton House he had its name changed to Orangefield, in admiration of King William of Orange. MacRae was such a fan of King William that he also gifted a statue of the king on horseback to the city of Glasgow. The original part of the house was a fairly typical classical box, the central portion with its pediment projecting beyond the main façade. The entrance was adorned with ionic pillars and rusticated quoins decorated the external edges of the building. The architect appears to be Samuel Neilson, a mason who also produced designs for country houses. At a later date wings were added to both sides of the house, echoing the classical appearance, but being slightly more decorative. Some of this work was by James Hay in 1906 and Thomson & Menzies of Glasgow in 1913. On the gables were Venetian windows, and at first-floor level were balustraded balconies, supported on the flat roofs of cellars. One of Orangefield's later owners was James Dalrymple, a friend and patron of Robert Burns, who was bankrupted in 1791 and died four years later. In 1933 Alex Mair was responsible for plans aimed at converting the house into a hotel. In 1943 the building was converted into the main terminal building for Prestwick Airport, the modern control tower being added to the roof of the original house. However, with the opening of the new airport control tower in 1962 and the building of the passenger terminal to plans by Joseph L. Gleave in 1964, the house was no longer required and it was cleared away in 1966.

SHEWALTON HOUSE

The site of Shewalton House, which stood to the west of Drybridge village, by the side of the River Irvine, has been changed completely, the lands converted into an industrial estate. The house was erected in 1806 for Colonel John Boyle in a plain Georgian style over two main floors, with an attic in the roofspace and other rooms in a semi-subterranean ground floor. The main front had a

Shewalton House.

simple entrance porch centrally placed in a recessed bay. To either side the bays advanced slightly, topped with hipped roofs. At some point in the life of the mansion a wing of similar style was added to the west. Anciently the lands were owned by the Fullartons, but in 1545 they passed to the Wallaces. The estate was later acquired by the Earl of Glasgow, and was lived on by Patrick Boyle, third son of the second Earl. His fourth, but only surviving, son, the Rt. Hon. David Boyle of Shewalton (1772–1853), inherited Shewalton in 1837. He became Lord Justice General and Lord President of the Court of Session in 1841. He was noted for his part in sentencing John Baird, Andrew Hardie and James Wilson, the political martyrs of the nineteenth century, as well as Burke and Hare, the infamous murderers. A statue of Boyle sculpted by John Steell was erected in Irvine's Castle Street in 1865. Shewalton House was demolished sometime early in the twentieth century.

TREARNE HOUSE

Standing to the east of Beith, Trearne was a large and rambling mansion built in the English baronial style in 1867 for William Ralston Patrick of Trearne, Hessilhead and Roughwood (d. 1919). It occupied the site of an earlier mansion that was no doubt too small for Ralston Patrick's aspirations. The architects employed to design the house were John Dick Peddie (1824–91) and Charles

Trearne House.

Kinnear, of Edinburgh. The main entrance was located in the base of a tall four-square tower of four storeys, topped by a battlemented viewing platform, from which 'an extensive panoramic view is commanded', according to John Shedden Dobie, writing in 1876. Each front of the house presented a number of gables of varying size, and there were a variety of single-storey bay windows. To the right of the main entrance block was an extensive wing. With decorative barge boards at the eaves, and contrasting quoins on the main corners and round the windows, the building was also adorned with string courses and armorial or monogrammed panels. After the Patricks, the MacFarlanes, of the MacFarlane and Lang biscuit manufacturers, owned Trearne. Following the First World War it served as Gresham House School for a time. Trearne was remodelled and refurbished at considerable expense internally around 1930, but this did not save the building, for it was demolished in 1954 to allow the extension of a limestone quarry nearby. The quarry virtually engulfed the whole of the former policies, leaving little to hint at former glories.

TREESBANKS HOUSE

The present Treesbanks House, which stands to the south of Riccarton at Kilmarnock, was erected in 1926–28 to the plans of James Carrick, at that time

Treesbanks House.

working in the office of James Kennedy Hunter of Ayr. Gavin Morton, of BMK, the Kilmarnock carpet manufacturer, built it. The house was erected on the site of a much older building, which was erected in three stages – the first was an ancient tower of indeterminate date to which the second stage was added in 1672 by James Campbell of Treesbanks, and the third in 1838 by George Campbell, 5th laird. James Campbell was the second son of Sir Hugh Campbell of Cessnock, and his father gave him the lands of Treesbanks in Riccarton parish, probably at the time of his marriage to Jean, a daughter of Mure of Rowallan. The Campbells remained at Treesbanks for over 200 years, and in fact claimed the chiefship of the Campbells of Loudoun once the Loudoun and Cessnock branches had become extinct. The house was a rather complicated mix of styles, and incorporated corbie-stepped gables, bay fronts, large Georgian windows and pediments. Within the grounds a brick doocot of 1771 survives, together the stable block of the former house, perhaps dating from the same time as the doocot.

WELLWOOD HOUSE

Wellwood was a rather large baronial house located to the west of Muirkirk. The Campbells owned the old house, which reputedly dated from 1600 and

Wellwood House.

was extended in 1740, until 1785. This was incorporated in a massive rebuilding of 1878, when Colonel John G.A. Baird (1854–1917) had a new country seat erected. He was the nephew of the noted ironmaster, James Baird, who purchased the 17,566-acre estate in 1863 for £135,000. What the nephew built, though baronial in essence, was rather plain, being devoid of turrets and crenellations, relying only on its bulk, string courses and corbie-stepped gables for effect. The main tower of the house was four storeys in height, and lesser blocks butted against it. Wellwood had a reputation for being haunted, and a female ghost named 'Beenie' was said to frequent a room in the original part of the house. She is reputed to have been a female who loved a man, but was murdered by a third party. A stone stairway in the house had what were claimed to be bloodstains on it and, despite many scrubbings by servants over the years, these could not be removed. A mason is supposed to have been given the job of replacing the stained step with a new one, but it is claimed that he mysteriously died shortly after the job was completed, and within a few days new bloodstains appeared. J.G.A. Baird was a keen historian, and produced a small book entitled *Muirkirk in Bygone Days*. The house was demolished in 1928, but the ornamental stonework of the imposing main entrance doorway was salvaged, only to be taken away by someone unknown.

CHAPTER 3

CHURCHES

ARDROSSAN
ST JOHN'S CHURCH

St John's Church stood in Ardrossan's Montgomerie Street, at the junction with Barr Street. The building was erected in 1859 as the town's Free Church. It was one of the works of the Glasgow architect, Campbell Douglas (1828–1910), who had produced plans for Alloway Parish Church the year previously. Ardrossan

St John's Parish Church in Ardrossan.

Free lacked the vitality and boldness of Alloway Church – perhaps the clients were not so well-heeled, and being adherents of the Free Church would rather have a simpler building. The main nave and chancel comprised plain ecclesiastical blocks, apparently all roof, the low walls being pierced by paired lancet windows to the east, and single lancets between buttresses to the west. The church tower was the saviour of the building as far as architecture goes, for it rose boldly, if somewhat squatly, from the street. Built in layers, the tower was roofed with a stone spire with lucarnes, but would have benefited from being at least half as tall again. Ardrossan Free Church became a United Free Church in 1900 and joined the Church of Scotland in 1929. The church was closed in September 1987 when the congregation merged with the Barony Church, and St John's was demolished as recently as 1991. Its site is now occupied by flats.

AYR
MORAVIAN CHURCH

The first Moravian brethren in Ayr were converted in 1765, when an Irishman, John Caldwell, arrived and began preaching to some of the locals. Moravians took their name from Moravia, from where the group sprang, passing through Bohemia and Saxony to Britain. They believed that all branches of Christianity should unite as one, and as such many of their adherents were often drawn from other churches, where they often remained in communion. The followers in Ayr formed a society in 1778 and within another couple of years had built themselves a place of worship in Mill Street, on the site of a malt kiln. This was erected to the rear of a house and from the street there was little sign of a place of worship. The Ayr church was the only Moravian church ever to exist in Scotland, and from it missionaries went to Irvine and Tarbolton to try to extend the group. In Irvine one of the adherents was the father of James Montgomery (1771–1854), who was to become famous as a hymn writer. His attempts at establishing a Moravian congregation there failed. The Ayr church was a simple preaching box; it was only obviously a church from its twin lancet windows and the fact that it had a small graveyard of its own. An upper floor in the church building was in 1816 converted into a schoolroom. In 1836 the church had around 200 members and in 1874 underwent some renovations. At one time the manse was adjoining the church, but in later years it was located at 2 Cassillis Street. Ayr Moravian Church closed in 1916 and the building was sold by the Moravian Union in 1945. The site was cleared a number of years later and is now occupied by blocks of flats dating from the 1970s.

The Moravian Church and tiny graveyard in Ayr.

AYR
ST JOHN'S CHURCH

The ancient church of St John the Baptist in Ayr was located on the edge of the town, west of the ancient main street now known as Sandgate. When the church was erected is not known, but it certainly existed as early as the thirteenth century, if not before. The earliest known reference to the building dates from 1233, when it is mentioned in the Paisley Abbey papers. The church had a large nave, north and south aisles, and north and south transepts. In plan it was cruciform in shape and had large gothic windows. At some point in the fifteenth century a tower was erected at the west end of the church, and it is this building that survives today as St John's Tower. Prior to the erection of the tower the church had a large rose window on the seaward gable, but this was susceptible to attack from the sea and damage from storms. The tower blocked this window off, which must have made the kirk far darker than the congregation was used to. The tower still stands four floors in height, dominating this

Top. The ancient church of St John's in Ayr,
as viewed from the sea in Slezer's view of 1693.
Above. The Wooden Kirk Mission, Ayr.

part of the town. The tower may have provided accommodation, for it contains an original fireplace, but it also housed two bells. The interior of the church was originally bare stone, but in 1613 this was covered with plaster and lime. In 1652 the land surrounding St John's was requisitioned for the construction of a massive fort by Oliver Cromwell, and the church found itself within the defences. A sum of money was granted to the congregation with which to build a new church – hence the present Auld Kirk of Ayr, located off High Street. The church was converted into an armoury at this time, and the tower was used as a ready-made lookout tower. In 1853 the old tower was sold to John Miller, who added to it and created a home that he called Fort Castle. The additions were planned by the architect John Murdoch. In 1914 Fort Castle was acquired by the Marquis of Bute and he stripped Miller's additions off the old tower and had it restored to its original appearance. The tower survives in a quiet area of greenery, and can be accessed at times.

AYR
WOODEN KIRK MISSION

Ayrshire, like the rest of Scotland, had many small evangelical and missionary groups. One of the most active was the Ayrshire Christian Union, and in 1881 it established a mission in Wallacetown, on the north side of the River Ayr. At first they met in a wooden hall, located in Limond's Wynd, off Cross Street, which locals were quick to name the 'Wooden Kirk'. Old photographs of it survive, depicting a wooden hall with large props supporting the side walls. The Wooden Kirk came to be its official name, and as the membership grew it was decided to erect a new mission hall. Built on the opposite, or east, side of the wynd, the new building was brick-built, and had little pretension to architecture, other than the angled bricks forming the lintels of the doors and windows, and the timbered gablet. The mission hall was opened for worship on 10 October 1898, as 'a comfortable place of worship for the poor of the district'. The architect was William MacClelland, who was responsible for a number of buildings in and around Ayr. The kirk had a large hall 36 feet by 30 feet, which could seat 221 persons, and a small hall of 24 feet by 14 feet, which could seat 94. The halls were separated by folding doors, allowing them to be formed into one large apartment. In addition there was a vestry or committee room, kitchen and toilet. The Christian Union gave up the hall and it was taken over as a mission hall by Newton Old Church in 1951, but it was demolished in January 1968.

BALLANTRAE
THE FREE CHURCH

The Free Church in Ballantrae was an attractive building, its tall spire dominating the small coastal community. At the Disruption, the adherents of the Free Church built a simple building for themselves around 150 yards north of the main road, near to the centre of the village, in what became known as Church Street. Local landowner, James MacIlwraith of Auchenflower laid the foundation stone on 18 April 1844. The church was opened on 20 December 1844 and had from 400 to 500 sittings. However, by 1876 the congregation had sufficient funds and benefactions to allow the erection of a new church. This was erected on what is known as Main Street East End. When the new place of worship was opened the old church was converted into a village hall, and served as such until a new hall was erected in 1928. The Free Church became a United Free charge in 1900, and on the union with the Church of Scotland in 1929 was given the name Ardstinchar Church. Soon after the union the congregations in Ballantrae merged again, and adopted the parish church as their base. This was a simple Gothic building of 1819, complete with a small but ornate clock tower on the east gable, added in 1891. The Free Church and Manse at Ballantrae were empty in 1931, and the church was demolished some time later.

BIRNIEKNOWE CHAPEL
AUCHINLECK

The official name for the Roman Catholic Chapel at Birnieknowe, east of Auchinleck, was Our Lady of Lourdes and St Patrick, but to most folk it was simply the 'Birnie Chapel'. The building stood by the side of the Auchinleck Burn, one mile or so east of the village, in an area that had a number of miners' rows, forming the village of Commondyke. At one time the chapel served a widespread congregation, for when it was built the priest there had to minister to folk in Mauchline, Catrine, Auchinleck and Cumnock. The church building was a very simple structure, with lancet windows along the side, a simple porch to the north and an apse to the south. Stone for it was quarried almost next to the chapel, and sand was dug from the stream. The building opened for worship in 1867, and eleven years later a school was added to the rear, also gone. Likewise the convent for the nuns, erected in 1885, has gone, though it survived for many years as a private house. The Birnieknowe Band was famous

Top. The Free Church in Ballantrae.
Above. Birnieknowe Chapel, near Auchinleck.

for many years for its skill in playing. In 1940, by when many of the miners had been rehoused in Auchinleck, the church had a hall erected in the village, but it was commandeered during the war and the church had little use of it. On the resumption of peace the hall came into its own, and from 1949 services could be held there. Fundraising efforts were now geared towards erecting a new chapel in Auchinleck, and the new church there was finally opened in June 1964. The Stations of the Cross, Sanctuary Lamp, font and pews were transferred from the old chapel and it was subsequently demolished in 1977. The school was closed in 1967, again being replaced by a new building in Auchinleck.

CUMNOCK FREE CHURCH

Little is known about the old Free Church of Cumnock. It was erected very soon after the Disruption of May 1843 when the Rev. Ninian Bannatyne left the Parish Church and established a free congregation in the town. The church was opened for worship on the last Sunday of October 1843 by a relative of the minister, the Rev. Archibald Bannatyne of Oban. The building was probably erected to one of the Free Church's standard plans that were produced nationally, and adapted locally, and therefore was most likely designed by David Cousin (1808–78) and William Gale. It had a triple roof, the gables of which faced onto Ayr Road. At

Cumnock Free Church.

the eaves were decorated barge boards and on the top of the tallest roof was an open belfry with weather vane. Built of random rubble, the church was distinguished by its rather small Venetian window at first floor level. The entrance door was reached through a round arch, a string course echoing the shape above it. The rest of the windows on the church were plain Georgian openings with lying panes. The church was taken down in the summer of 1896 to clear a site in order to build the present church building, erected to plans by David Menzies of Edinburgh. Menzies is noted as being the restorer, to some extent unsuccessfully, of Plean Tower, which stands to the south east of Stirling. The new church, which is a major landmark in the town, was known as the Crichton Memorial Church, having been the gift of the Crichton family, but from 2004 has been renamed Old Cumnock Trinity Church.

CUMNOCK PARISH CHURCH

A growing community resulted in the loss of Cumnock's old parish church in 1863, though as early as 1837 different plans were being considered for its replacement. The church building, which stood where the present Old Church

The old Adam parish church that stood in Cumnock Square.

occupies the centre of The Square, had become too small for the congregation, and the benevolence of the 3rd Marquis of Bute resulted in it being pulled down and replaced by a Victorian Gothic building, designed by James Maitland Wardrop of Edinburgh. The original church had also been the gift of the same family, at that time titled Earl of Dumfries, heritor of the parish, and it was erected in 1754 to replace an even older building, of which no illustration seems to survive. The brothers John and Robert Adam were employed to design the church – they were working on Lord Dumfries' new mansion a few miles west of the town at the time – and it was one of their few ecclesiastical designs. The main building was single-storey in height, and basically was T-shaped in plan, but with a bell tower to the south side, making it cruciform. The windows were large arched openings, with simple timber astragals, and these had exterior shutters, closed when the ancient sport of handball was played in the Square. On one of the walls was affixed the jougs, an iron neck-ring used to imprison malefactors. The church tower was rather squat in appearance, and contained an old bell cast in 1697 by Quirinus de Visscher of Rotterdam. The tower contained a public clock, and over this were four large ball finials at the corners. A stone spire rose above this. The church could originally accommodate 700 worshippers, but in 1822 internal alterations were carried out, at which time the internal stairs were removed and replaced by external stone steps, leading to balconies. These steps became used for local hustings and public meetings.

DALMELLINGTON
ST BARBARA'S R.C. CHURCH

Our Lady and St Barbara, to give the church its full title, was one of a number of modern churches built in the early 1960s to serve a congregation that had moved from old miners' rows or inner-town slums into new housing estates. St Barbara's was built on the hill in Dalmellington, and it was planned that it would serve the Catholics of the upper Doon valley, replacing the older church of St Xavier's, which was located at the old steelworks village of Waterside. The church was erected between 1959 and 1961, opening for worship on 9 April that year, the dedication service being led by the Rev. Dr Joseph McGee of Ayr. St Barbara's was different in style to the usual ecclesiastical buildings and was typical of the Roman Catholic Church in designing modern places of worship. The architect was Charles W. Gray of Edinburgh, who designed a number of Roman Catholic churches. Basically octagonal in plan, the church had gables on

Dalmellington: St Barbara's R.C. Church.

each face, the roofs terminating in a central fleche. On some façades there were various short wings or apses. Gray was to design other octagonal chapels, such as St Teresa's in Craigmillar, Edinburgh, erected in 1963. St Barbara's cost £17,000 to erect, and it could accommodate 250 worshippers. The Catholics of the Doon valley never did unite in this building, and St Xavier's Church continued to be used by a separate congregation. At length St Barbara's adherents joined with St Xavier's and St Barbara's was abandoned. The building suffered from vandalism for a number of years until it was demolished on 12 July 2003.

DALRY PARISH CHURCH

The old parish church of Dalry was erected in 1771 on the site of an older place of worship, itself believed to have been erected around 1604. The church was a fairly plain building, with two storeys of windows, no doubt due to balconies within. According to Pont's *Cunninghame Topographised*, the church was 'a typical heritor's building, plain and quadrilateral, as devoid of any architectural adornment as the most humble dwelling within the sound of its bell'. Built of rubble, the church had few means of ornament, other than a Venetian window at one end, and a small bell tower at the other. This was not actually attached to the church building, other than by means of an external stairway. The bell tower had been part of the earlier church and was retained when a larger place of worship was erected, capable of seating 870. It is thought that the

Top. Dalry Parish Church.
Above. St Andrew's Church, Dalry.

church cost £277 10s to build. The parish church underwent considerable repair in 1821, when new cast iron pillars were installed to replace the old wooden ones that supported the galleries and roof. This produced a much improved interior. However, in 1837 the minister noted that the walls were 'rent and forced outwards, while the roof has bent inward'. It was to survive for only another fifty years. In 1870 the heritors decided to erect a new church, the present St Margaret's Parish Church, on the same site, to plans by David Thomson (c. 1830–1910). This place of worship, which cost £4,500 to build, is dominated by its tall spire of 159 feet and was erected between 1871 and 1873.

DALRY
ST ANDREW'S U.F. CHURCH

Originally built as a Free Church, St Andrew's dates from shortly after the Disruption, perhaps around 1845. Built in New Street, the church was a fairly small building, its gable facing the street. Atop this was a belfry which was rather large for the building, the weight of it being held on corbels over the gable, spreading the weight to either side of the windows. It contained a circular panel, as if for a clock, but there does not ever seem to have been one. The main windows were plain glassed tripartite lancets, over which a simple moulding formed a drip. Above this was a panel with a representation of the burning bush. There were two doorways into the church, and these were located in a separate block to either side of the main gable. These doors were arched, again with hoodmoulds, and over these were paired lancet windows. On top of the smaller gables were carved finials. Adjacent to the church was the Free Church School, but this was later to be used as the infant department of the parish school. The church was to become a United Free Church in 1900, taking the name St Andrew's. The congregation later joined the Church of Scotland (in 1929), but the church was closed in 1962. The building was demolished soon afterwards, although the former school building survives and is now the village post office.

DALRYMPLE FREE CHURCH

After the Disruption, the villagers of Dalrymple who left the parish church held their services by the riverside, the minister preaching from the back of a cart. After a short period of time, the congregation met in a shed at Mr Watt's

Dalrymple Free Church.

smithy, but in 1863 the simple Gothic building shown here was erected at the junction of Barbieston and Burnton roads, at the east end of the village. The foundation stone was laid on 22 July that year, and within a year a church capable of holding 300 worshippers was erected. The tall lancet windows and the simply belfry were all that adorned the building, which could quite simply be a domestic dwelling otherwise. The parishioners added a manse in 1868 and a hall in 1898. At the Union of 1929 the church was named Dalrymple Saint Valley, to distinguish it from the old parish church, but in 1936 the church was closed and used for a time as a house. It was later demolished (apart from a low wall) and rebuilt with the former manse as the present White Horse Inn.

DARNCONNER PARISH CHURCH

Darnconner is a lost mining village that was located on the moors to the north east of Auchinleck. Today there are only a farm house and two cottages in existence where at one time there was a thriving community of miners' rows, school, co-op and church. The latter started off its life as a corrugated iron shed,

Darnconner Parish Church with manse to the right.

erected in 1874 and described as 'more airy than comfortable', until it was blown down in a storm. In its place a new gothic-styled church was erected with funds provided by Robert Angus of Craigston, the local mine manager. The architect was Robert Samson Ingram (1840–1915), and the building he produced was a rather simple yet dignified structure, built of Ballochmyle sandstone and topped with a simple belfry. Internally the church had a nave, small transepts and a chancel, the latter floored with small tiles. The interior of the church had Kilwinning freestone dressings. Adjoining the church building was the manse, and this is one of the cottages that survives. The church, which cost £3,000 to build, could accommodate 300 worshippers, and it was opened on 14 March 1897 when the Auchinleck parish ministers, the Rev. Dr James Chrystal and the Rev. James Hill, conducted a service jointly. Only one wedding was ever conducted in the church, and with the removal of the miners' rows and the rehousing of the occupants in Auchinleck, the church was closed in 1939. The pews were removed for use in Auchinleck parish church, which had suffered a major fire; the bell was removed to Catrine Congregational Church and the font to Auchinleck Peden Church. The building remained standing until it was demolished in 1979.

DREGHORN
CONGREGATIONAL CHURCH

Dreghorn E.U. Congregational Church dated from 1904, being opened on 20 May that year by the Rev. George Gladstone of Glasgow. The congregation had been founded in 1864 and joined the Evangelical Union in 1865. They originally met in a small cottage or shop located at the east end of the village, which held 100 worshippers. The congregation thrived, and were able to afford to build a new place of worship in 1864–65, when a new church was erected further down Main Street. This was a rather simple building, but again the congregation raised funds and 40 years later were able to erect a third church, located on the opposite side of Main Street. The new church could accommodate 450 worshippers, but the architect seems to be unknown. The church had a large geometric traceried window facing south, the walls having rusticated masonry. A number of buttresses supported the walls, and ashlar was used for quoins. Some of these had heavy chamfers. The church was rather idiosyncratic in appearance, with smooth masonry on high gables, a truncated tower awaiting another fundraising revival that never materialised, and heavy skew putts

Dreghorn Congregational Church.

supporting skewstones. The church was noted for its internal woodwork, and a pipe organ that was installed at a cost of £210, half of which was paid for by Dr Carnegie. A declining congregation meant that the church was closed for worship in 1986. The building was used as a workshop and store for many years, but it was eventually demolished as recently as 2003.

GIRVAN PARISH CHURCH

The old parish church in Girvan was a simple, yet dignified building. It stood at the top of Hamilton Street and was erected in 1780. The church was similar in style to the old kirk that survives in Fenwick, with tall lancet windows on the gables, and plain Georgian windows on the adjoining walls. Beneath the lancet windows were doors giving access to the church, some of which were private doors used by the local heritors. Only the little belfry atop one of the gables was an additional feature. The church was taken down in 1883 when the present parish church was erected in Montgomerie Street to replace it, the work of the architect, William Gardner Rowan (1845–1924). Prior to the demolition of the church, the building had degenerated into a poor condition. The Rev. Roderick Lawson (1831–1907) could remember the church as it was in his youth. It had an

The old parish church at Girvan.

'earthen floor, the narrow pews guiltless of paint, the old pulpit with precentor's desk in front, putting one in mind of the bow of a two-decker, and which, when I was latterly permitted to preach in it, I found to be so deep that I had to place one stool on top of another to make myself visible. I can remember, too, the last minister of it remarking to some members of Presbytery who were visiting it: "The state of this church speaks for itself." "Yes," was the reply, 'it is *of age*, and has a full right to do so.'"

GLENBUCK PARISH CHURCH

Designed by Robert Ingram, the church at Glenbuck was built to serve a once-thriving community of 1,750 residents. Glenbuck village was established as a result of the foundation of ironworks and the associated mining for coal and ironstone. The church was erected at the expense of the Bairds and was opened for worship on 16 July 1882. It was a simple Gothic building, with three lancets on the gable, over which was a small open belfry with bell. Below this was a lozenge bearing the Church of Scotland symbol. The entrance doorway was located to one side. Glenbuck church was reduced in status in 1946 and was united with Muirkirk Parish Church on 13 May 1953. The church was finally closed in May 1954 when Charles Horn, the last ordained missionary of the church, conducted a closing service. The building stood for a number of years thereafter, until it was finally demolished. At that time a large slab bearing an inscription in memory of the local Covenanters was removed and relocated in Muirkirk churchyard.

KAMES PARISH CHURCH

Kames Parish Church was erected between 1903 and 1904 from red sandstone. The cost of the building was met by Messrs William Baird & Co. Ltd, as was the manse. The mason work was carried out by George Reid & Son of Catrine, the joinery work by John Wood of Muirkirk. The church opened for worship on 31 January 1904 by the Right Rev. John Gillespie, Moderator of the Church of Scotland. The architect was Robert Ingram, who designed the building in a Gothic style. Built of red sandstone, it had a white stone finish internally. The organ was the gift of William Weir of Adamton, and the chancel window commemorated Robert Angus's son. Ingram himself gifted the pulpit cloth, collection bags and baptismal font. The church lasted for less than fifty

Top. Glenbuck Parish Church and war memorial.
Above. Kames Parish Church.

years as a place of worship, for the old miners' rows on the south side of Muirkirk were gradually cleared away and the church was closed on 7 December 1952, the service led by the Rev. Chris Jack and the Rev. C. Horn. The stained glass window and many of the pews from the church were removed and incorporated in the parish church in Muirkirk (erected in 1812 to plans by William Stark), which had suffered a serious fire in 1949 and was being restored. The church itself was demolished in 1957.

KILMARNOCK
CLERK'S LANE CHURCH

Clerk's Lane in Kilmarnock is a long-lost thoroughfare that has succumbed to concrete and tarmacadam, now being buried below the multistorey car park and surrounding parking areas between Green Street and Foregate. At one time the street linked Regent Street (which formed its western continuation) and New and Green streets. In this lane stood one of those typically Scottish 'box kirks', so beloved of the Secessionists, where ornamentation in archi-

Kilmarnock: Clerk's Lane Church.

tecture was anathema, and churches were buildings to be preached at within, and not admired without. The Anti-Burgher branch of the Associate Presbytery built the original Clerk's Lane Church in 1775, but in 1807 it was rebuilt in a larger format. It comprised a typical rectangular box, adorned externally by arched windows at first floor, or balcony level. Writing in 1898, Thomas Smellie noted that, 'it was possessed of little architectural beauty, but a certain quaint charm attached to the old-world surroundings of the chapel, with its square porches and sentry box, where stood the watchful guardian of the "plate".' Inside there were seats for 1,000 adherents, and at one time its minister the Rev. James Robertson (d. 1811) was so popular that they were often filled. Indeed, when the Rev. Dr Mackinlay of the Laigh Kirk was absent on business, many of his congregation were wont to attend Clerk's Lane Church. On one occasion their arrival disturbed Robertson at prayer, whereupon he responded, 'Sit roun', sit roun', my frien's, and gi'e the fleein' army room; for their wee bit idol, ye ken, is no at hame the day.' In 1841 the congregation split over the teachings of the Rev. James Morison, and 40 of the congregation withdrew to form ultimately the Princes Street U.P. Church. The Morisonians continued in Clerk's Lane Church, becoming linked with other congregations to form the Evangelical Union, but they removed in 1860 with the erection of a new place of worship. Clerk's Lane Church closed in 1907 and in 1911 was converted into the Electric Cinema. The cinema closed in 1938 and the building was eventually demolished.

KILMARNOCK
GLENCAIRN CHURCH

Glencairn Church was one of those many church buildings that existed in towns across Scotland and when their usefulness had passed were either demolished or converted for other uses. In Glencairn's case, both outcomes were used, after it had ceased to function as a church, for it survived a number of years until it was demolished in 1993, to allow for the extension of an adjoining factory. The church building, which was of a typical Gothic style, was erected in 1881 as the Holm U.P. Church, replacing an earlier mission hall on the same site, which itself replaced an earlier building on the opposite side of West Shaw Street, just off Glencairn Square. The mission here was established in 1873 by the Rev. James Banks, who came from Glasgow and did much of his ministry with the working classes at this end of the town. He was instrumental in educating his congregation, teaching English, Hebrew and Greek. The

Top. Glencairn Church, Kilmarnock.
Above. King Street Church, Kilmarnock.

church was the work of Robert Baldie, of Baldie & Tennant of Glasgow. In 1900 the U.P. Church nationally joined with the Free Church to form the United Free Church, and this congregation was renamed Glencairn U.F. until 1929, when it became part of the Church of Scotland. The church congregation was linked with St Andrew's Church in 1954 and was united with it in 1967, after which the building became redundant. St Andrew's Church itself closed for worship in 2002.

KILMARNOCK
KING STREET CHURCH

One of the most prominent landmarks in Kilmarnock succumbed to the developer in 1966. King Street Church had been closed and the congregation were to join the Portland Road Church and be rehoused in the modern Howard Church in Portland Road, erected in 1970–71. The site was used for modern shop premises, built with a steel frame with brick infill. King Street Church had been erected in 1832, when it was a Relief Church. The congregation had its origins in 1799 when it broke away from Riccarton Parish Church over the patron of the parish refusing them a choice of minister. At first they met in a barn in Riccarton, but in 1802 they built a meeting house there. The Rev. James Kirkwood was inducted in 1811, and so popular a minister was he that the congregation outgrew the hall. As many Kilmarnock parishioners had now joined the congregation, it was decided to build a new church in King Street in 1814, opening in 1816. This again became too small, and in 1832 the King Street Relief Church was built on the same site, with sittings for almost 1,500. The building cost over £4,000 to build. Designed by Robert Johnston, or Johnstone as it has sometimes been spelt, the building was dominated by its 120-foot-tall spire, paid for by subscription at a cost of £800. This steeple contained the largest brass bell in the town, one that was so loud that it could be heard throughout Kilmarnock, and it was noted that when the conditions were right, it could also be heard in a number of surrounding villages. The spire also contained a clock with four faces, the mechanism of which was the work of Breckenridge & Son of Kilmarnock. According to Archibald Mackay, writing in 1880, 'this, we may remark, was the second dissenting church in Scotland on which a steeple was erected, and the first, we believe, from which issued the sounds of the Sabbath-bell.' The church was opened on 14 April 1833. In 1847 the congregation joined the United Presbyterian Church and later became a congregation of the Church of Scotland.

KILMARNOCK
ST ANDREW'S NORTH CHURCH

St Andrew's North Church was originally a Free Church congregation that broke away from St Andrew's Church, which still stands in St Andrew's Street, but which is now secular. The Free St Andrew's Church was built in Fowlds Street in 1844 at a cost of £1,200. It had 930 seats for the congregation and the first minister was the Rev. Neil Brodie. The architect of the original building is unknown, and it was probably erected to the Free Church's standard plans. In 1883 the church was bursting at the seams and it was proposed to sell the building and erect a new church and halls elsewhere. However, it was decided to extend the existing building, and Robert Ingram provided plans for this. Work was done in 1886, creating a new rose window on the street gable, and the original entrance was closed off. A large belfry was erected to one side, containing the new entrance and double gallery stairs. The interior was rebuilt and a new lecture hall was added to the rear. The cost of the alterations was £2,483 1s 1d. The large belfry was more like a classical temple than a typical ecclesiastical spire. It had a two-storey four-square base, over which a classical campanile towered, the four fronts having pillars and a pediment surrounding the louvred openings of the belfry, the whole topped by a cylindrical finial. The church was demolished in 1986 to allow the construction of shop premises by Bett developments.

KILWINNING ABBEY

Although there are quite significant remains of Kilwinning Abbey still standing in the old churchyard, there are parts of the abbey that were known to exist and of which only drawings survive. The present tower, which stands isolated from the ruins and parish church, was built to replace an older tower. In the engraving shown here, the old tower is seen to the right, rising through three floors and topped with a simple corbie-stepped hipped roof. This was one of two towers, which flanked the west end of the nave. Only the foundations of the south tower survive. The northern tower was struck by lightning on 2 August 1809, causing considerable damage to it. The tower remained in a precarious condition for some time, but in 1814 massive blocks of masonry collapsed, and what was left was deemed so dangerous that it was blown up with gunpowder. It was noted that the stone was 'rooted out even to the foundations, so that not a single stone is now left to indicate either its

Top. St Andrew's North Church, Kilmarnock.
Above. Kilwinning Abbey from an early engraving.

position or character.' In 1815 a new tower was erected to plans drawn up by David Hamilton. He copied the basic shape of the original, with a larger window on the first floor, divided into two lancets, and paired windows on the top floor. Between, Hamilton had room to add a public clock. Kilwinning was one of the finest abbeys in Scotland, very distinctive in its architecture, with many features not seen elsewhere. It was a Tironensian foundation, dating from 1187, and its nave and transepts were wider than even Glasgow Cathedral or Paisley Abbey. In length it was only 225 feet, which was shorter than most other abbeys. The abbey is said to have been established by Richard or Hugh Morville, who is thought to have fled here following the murder of Thomas à Becket. He was granted the lordship of Cuninghame and was Great Constable of Scotland. The abbey was abandoned at the Reformation, and became a quarry for stone for local buildings. A number of houses were also created out of some of the ruins, and for many years these survived attached to the ruins. One of these is shown in the sketch, a vernacular block of perhaps three or four storeys, the roof having the traditional corbie-stepped gables.

MAUCHLINE NORTH CHURCH

The origins of the North Church go back to the Burgher adherents who met in the Meeting House. This was a typical Scots 'preaching box', unadorned externally and easily mistaken for a normal house, other than the fact that it

Mauchline North Church.

84

had two tall arched, but clear-glassed, windows. The first minister was the Rev. John Walker, who remained for 37 years. The church became connected with the United Presbyterian Church. The original Meeting House was demolished in 1884 and on the same site a new church building was erected at a cost of £2,500. This was named the Walker Memorial Church after Rev. Walker. The architects of the new Gothic building were Robert Baldie & William Tennant of Glasgow, and Alexander Hyslop of Mauchline erected the building. In 1896 the Ayr architect, James A. Morris, made some site inspections at the church, but it is not known for what reason. Perhaps the manse was erected around this time. In 1925 the Abbey Church in Mauchline united with the Walker Memorial Church and was renamed the North Church. Following another union with the parish church in 1975 the church was closed, and was used for a number of years as a store. It was demolished in 1983 and a house now occupies the site.

MAYBOLE
CARGILL CHURCH

The Disruption of the Church of Scotland and the formation of the Free Church resulted in hundreds of new church buildings being built all over Scotland. In

Maybole: Cargill Church.

Maybole the dissenters were not long in having their own Free Church erected at the top of Barns Road in the village, and this opened for worship in 1844. To distinguish the church from the parish church, the Free Church was named the Cargill Church, in honour of the noted Covenanter, Donald Cargill, who preached nearby in 1681. A large boulder, which became known as the Cargill Stone, marked the spot of his conventicle, and part of this was incorporated in the Free Church building. A hall was added to the rear in 1882. There were triple lancets on each gable, and high on some walls were pedimented wallhead dormers. On 30 December 1906 the church building went on fire, and the fire brigade was blamed for the building being virtually lost, although they blamed the cold weather for freezing the water supply. In any case the building was reduced to a shell, only the cylindrical belfry and the church hall surviving. The congregation, by now a United Free Church, had the church rebuilt, and it was at this time the porch was added and a new large window installed in the rear wall. On 6 July 1949 the congregation united with the Kincraig church and the building was renamed the Cargill-Kincraig church. In 1979 the building was demolished and houses were erected on the site. The Cargill stone was relocated to near the new houses in 2004.

Left. Kincraig Church, Maybole.
Right. Muirkirk U.P. Church.

MAYBOLE
KINCRAIG CHURCH

The Kincraig Church in Maybole was originally a United Presbyterian place of worship and was erected in Culzean Road in 1880. It replaced the old burgher kirk building that stood elsewhere in the village and which dated from 1797. Kincraig Church was probably the most attractive of Maybole's churches, having some pretensions to decent architecture. The building was constructed of red sandstone, and was distinguished by its tall stone steeple. This rose from a heavily buttressed square tower, with set-back buttresses, the entrance doorway of which was located at the foot of it. On an upper level was a louvred bell room, over which was a broach spire. On the main front was a traceried window, with four panels containing stained glass. In style the building was not unlike work by the Ayr architect, John Murdoch. Unfortunately, when the congregation was united with the Cargill congregation, the latter church was kept and the Kincraig building was sold to a developer, who demolished it and erected houses on the site.

MUIRKIRK U.P. CHURCH

The United Presbyterian Church in Muirkirk was established when the Secession Church and the Relief Church merged. A new church was erected in the village's Main Street in 1823 and the first minister, the Rev. James Garret, was inducted the following year. The church was a basic shell, with Gothic pointed arched windows. Only the gable, which faced the Main Street, was built of dressed masonry, and was adorned with a slightly projecting door surround and a small open belfry. In 1900 the U.P. church nationally merged with the Free Church to create the United Free Church. Muirkirk also had a Free Church, and so the two new U.F. congregations were named Chalmers U.F. (in the former Free Church) and the Muirkirk Main Street U.F. Church (in the former U.P. building). The two churches were united in 1915 and the Main Street Church was converted into the church hall, known as the Dundas Hall, after the last minister there, the Rev. John Dundas. When the U.F. Church merged with the Church of Scotland in 1929 Muirkirk ended up with too many church buildings, and the hall was sold. James Muir converted it into a picture-house, opening on 2 December 1938 as the Regal Cinema. The little belfry was removed, the façade was rebuilt in rendered brick and the arched windows were filled in. Within were seats for 600 and the murals on the walls were

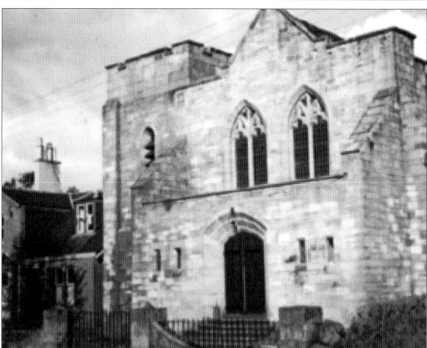

Top. New Cumnock: Afton Church.
Above. New Cumnock: Bank Church.

notable for their local scenes. The cinema only lasted for two months before burning down in February, and it did not reopen again until July 1939 following a refit. The cinema was closed on 18 July 1970 and was demolished in June 1972.

NEW CUMNOCK
AFTON CHURCH

The Afton Church in New Cumnock was a rather small building, but was of a better architectural quality than many smaller places of worship. The congregation was a Reformed Presbyterian one, formed by the remnants of the Covenanters who refused to return to the Church of Scotland after the Glorious Revolution. One of the ministers, the Rev. Matthew Hutcheson, was a popular preacher, and also author of a history of the United Presbyterian Church and editor of *The Martyr Graves of Scotland*. He raised funds for a new church, which was erected in 1868 on a sizeable plot of ground at the junction of Mason Avenue with Afton Bridgend. Within the plot the manse was also erected. Built of random rubble on three walls, the main gable facing the street was more decorative, having angled buttresses and black whinstone walls. The windows were surrounded with light coloured sandstone and were glazed with simple Georgian panes, the borders of which had red or blue coloured glass. High on the gable was a trefoil shaped ventilator. Within were seats for a congregation of 300. At first the church was a United Presbyterian place of worship, but in 1900 it became a United Free church, taking the name Afton Church. In 1923 the congregation merged with the Arthur Memorial U.F. Church, the final service being taken by the Rev. John Warrick of Cumnock on 11 November. The Afton church was then used as a Masonic temple by the local Masonic Lodge, and as a sale room, before being taken over by the Brethren and renamed the Bridgend Gospel Hall, serving as such for a number of years. In 1976 the church was demolished when the Brethren built themselves a new meeting hall.

NEW CUMNOCK
BANK CHURCH

The Bank Church was erected at the mining village of Bank Glen, to the south west of New Cumnock, in 1898–1900. The congregation was formed in 1873 when a mission of the Free Church was established here, meeting in a tin building. Bank Free Church's Band of Hope was founded in October 1897 with a membership of 140. With a growing membership and funds, a new building was erected to replace the tin kirk. The foundation stone, which was rescued when the church was demolished, survives, and is now to be seen at the former manse. It is inscribed *AMDC This stone of Bank Free Church was laid April 22 1899*. In 1900 it became a United Free Church, and the manse was located to the north east of the church building. Bank Church was a rather solid-looking structure, heavily shouldered with a squat tower. The building seemed to have rather small windows for the size of it. It was designed very much in what has become known as the Glasgow style, made famous by Charles Rennie Mackintosh. Even the inscribed foundation stone of the church has been carved with a font that hints at Mackintosh's style of lettering, with a raised O and flattened angles on the Ns. In 1960 the church was closed, the congregation being united with the parish church. Bank Church was demolished in the summer of 1961.

NEW CUMNOCK FREE CHURCH

The Free Church in New Cumnock was erected soon after the Disruption, when the local minister, the Rev. Matthew Kirkland, left the parish church. He was instrumental in raising funds for a new church, which was erected from

New Cumnock Free Church.

local whinstone. The site for the building was on the mound of what was Cumnock Castle, known also as Black Bog Castle, from its location in the midst of what had been an island in a loch, latterly a bog. The building was very similar to the old Free Church in Cumnock, already mentioned, with the triple gables and arched string course. Adjoining were a school and a manse, added within a few years. Like Cumnock, this church was demolished to allow for the erection of a grander building, the donation of a rich benefactor and supporter of the Free Church, by this time United Free. In 1912 the church was taken down and the Arthur Memorial United Free Church was erected in its place. This was built of rich yellow sandstone to plans by the Welsh architect, W. Beddoes Rees, perhaps his only work in Scotland. The Arthur Memorial Church was closed in 1982 and has stood rather unsure of itself, above New Cumnock village ever since.

NEWMILNS
LOUDOUN EAST CHURCH

The Free Church in Newmilns had been formed in the village's Sun Inn on 30 June 1845. The village was late to join the Free Church movement, for until then they had been happy with the minister presented by the local laird.

Newmilns: Loudoun East Church.

However, when he moved on the congregation was split over the merits of the new minister, and a free congregation was established. Within a few months the congregation had managed to raise sufficient funds to allow the erection of a fairly simple Gothic building, built in what was at the time open countryside above the main village in King Street. The foundation stone was laid on 10 March 1846 by William Howieson Craufurd of Craufurdland Castle. The architect is unknown, but the mason work was carried out by James Anderson, the wright work by J. & T. Hood, plasterwork by Kinloch & Elder, slating by John Lawson and plumbing by Lawson of Kilmarnock. The building was located back from the road, and an avenue of trees led to the front door. Over the arched doorway were three lancet windows, and on the top of the gable was a small belfry. This had been an afterthought, for when the church was under construction it was pointed out that a small belfry would cost another £42, and this was quickly raised. A further £29 was raised by Andrew Mair to cover the cost of a bell. The total cost of building the church was calculated to be £864 7s. 10½d, but gratis work and donations of materials had kept this figure low. The church united again with Loudoun Parish Church in 1980 and the building was demolished in 1983.

NEWTON-UPON-AYR OLD CHURCH

Erected in 1777, Newton-upon-Ayr Old Parish Church was one of the most dignified buildings in the town. Erected by the Freemen of Newton, it was originally a chapel-of-ease to prevent the residents from having to attend the church in Monkton, 3½ miles to the north. It was raised to full status in 1779. The building cost £2,000 to erect, and was extended slightly in the 1830s, bringing the number of parishioners it could accommodate up to 1,032. A simple classical building, it did not have all the trappings of later church buildings, and stood rather isolated in its small graveyard. On the north side of the building was a square aisle, but the three other sides, including the two gables, had semicircular apses. Adorned by simple arched windows with plain glass, originally the church could seat 830 worshippers. The church was reached by passing through the archway at the foot of the Newton Steeple, part of the burgh tolbooth, which itself was saved when the rest was cleared away. In 1962 the Old Church and Newton New Church (which was erected in 1862 to plans by William Clarke) were united. A campaign to save the old building failed, despite a public inquiry, and it was demolished in 1963 to allow the wide carriageway of King Street to be created.

Newton-upon-Ayr Old Church.

OCHILTREE FREE CHURCH

The Free Church in Ochiltree was erected soon after the Disruption, at the instigation of the Rev. Joseph Patrick (1814–71), who was to serve in the church for 27 years. Built on rising ground above the newer roadway to Ayr, at the junction with the narrow Doctor's Road, the church was a rather simple building, probably built to one of the Free Church's standard plans. The main block was a simple preaching box; the side walls adorned with tall arched windows with plainly glazed panes. On the gable facing the roadway the church had more of an attempt at architectural styling, with arched windows containing hoodmoulds, and a central belfry. The church suffered in a fire in January 1924 but was restored shortly afterwards. In February 1928 the pipe organ that was formerly located within the New Cumnock U.F. Church was donated to the church and installed. After the union of the United Free and Established Church in 1929 this church became known as Ochiltree South Church. It was closed on 6 March 1935. In 1939 the bell from the tower was removed and gifted to Lochside Parish Church in Ayr, which was being built as an extension charge in the town. The old church at Ochiltree was demolished in 1967. The village war memorial, which formerly stood at the junction of Main Street with Ayr Road, was relocated to the site of the church.

Ochiltree Free Church.

PERCETON & DREGHORN
PARISH CHURCH

The Perceton and Dreghorn parish church is not technically lost. We know where it is! The building now stands in Japan, having been dismantled stone by stone and shipped halfway around the world. It is now located at a hotel which offers wedding ceremonies. The Japanese wanted a Christian church, in particular one that looked sufficiently ecclesiastical, and one where the main aisle led from the front door to the pulpit, to allow brides to march to the altar in the traditional way. The stained glass windows were removed in their entirety, and the roof trusses lifted off complete. The stones were numbered and dismantled, and the whole sent in packing crates to Japan in 1997. The church was originally erected at the eastern end of Dreghorn, half way to Springside, by the Free Church in 1877. The architect of both the church and manse (which survives as a private house) was Robert Baldie. A rather fine

Left. Perceton & Dreghorn Parish Church.
Right. St Nicholas Church, Prestwick.

building, the church was Gothic in style, with a tall spire at the left side of the main north gable. This changed in plan from square to octagonal, and finished in a stone-built campanile. The church became a United Free Church in 1900 and joined the Church of Scotland in 1929. The former manse still stands to its western side; the Congregational Church manse was located to its east.

PRESTWICK
ST NICHOLAS CHURCH

The ruins of the ancient kirk of St Nicholas in Prestwick still stand on a low knoll in the town, surrounded by its graveyard. The church was established sometime in the twelfth century, when Prestwick was created a Burgh of Barony, but it may occupy a much older site. At that time the church is thought to have been a timber structure. In the thirteenth century the church was rebuilt in stone, a simple edifice with little ornamentation. The illustration, drawn in 1834, shows the church still sporting a roof. How much of the early church of the thirteenth century was incorporated in the building of that time is unknown, but the windows do not appear to be particularly old, being simple Georgian style. Two moulded capitals of the early period survive. Perhaps only part of a longer aisle was roofed, the remainder demolished. One gable, which may have been an original one, had buttresses, and on the apex was a small belfry. The bell, which was cast in Holland in 1619, is now located at Kingcase School. The church was abandoned in 1837 when the new parish church, serving both Monkton and Prestwick was built, located halfway between the two communities. From that time the church roof was removed, and the walls robbed for stones. Today the walls are incomplete, and the dressed stone has been removed.

RICCARTON RELIEF CHURCH

In the eighteenth century there were a number of schisms in the Church of Scotland, and various secession churches were established. The Original Secession took place in 1733 and the second secession, which resulted in the creation of Relief Churches, occured in 1761. Thomas Gillespie, the minister of Carnock in Fife, and others left the Church of Scotland and set up their own church, 'for the relief of Christians oppressed in their Christian privileges'. The main difficulty they had was concerning the rights of the local landowner or patron over the church. In Riccarton a number of people decided to leave the parish church in 1799 when the local patron refused to give them their choice of minister. They soon allied themselves with the Relief Presbytery of Glasgow. At first they worshipped in a barn at Riccarton, but in 1802 they were able to erect

Riccarton Relief Church.

a meeting-house, as many of their churches were originally called, at the corner of Hurlford Road. At the same time they appointed their first minister, the Rev. Daniel MacNaught. The Free Church building was typical of many seceders' churches. They were usually devoid of any architectural ornament, and were more akin to Scots domestic architecture. Riccarton Relief Church appeared like a double-storey house, and would be indistinguishable from one were it not for its twin arched windows at first-floor level over the main entrance. Most of the windows of the church were protected with wooden shutters. The second minister of the church was the Rev. James Kirkwood. He was such a gifted preacher that he attracted a large following, and in 1814 it was decided that a larger church was required. By this time most of the congregation came from Kilmarnock, so it was decided to erect a new church there, at the corner of King Street and St Marnock Street. The site of this building was later occupied by the King Street Church of 1832, which has also been demolished.

SALTCOATS LANDSBOROUGH CHURCH

Originally built as Saltcoats Free Church in 1843, this church was erected on a site on Findlay's Brae, between Nineyards Street and Seaview Road. The congregation had planned building on a site midway between Saltcoats and

Saltcoats: Landsborough Church, prior to the addition of the steeple.

Stevenston, but the proprietor refused to sell the site. Instead the site in Saltcoats was built on, the ground having been gifted by Dr Dow of Greenock. His father had been minister of Ardrossan parish church from 1739–87, and he was willing to gift the land, 'for the sake of the guid auld kirk, and the good old man and his father, who had long been a minister of that kirk'. The oldest part of the church was opened for worship in January 1844, the architect being David Cousin (1808–1878) of Edinburgh. The original building was found to be too small for the congregation's needs, so in 1869 Robert Baldie of Glasgow was commissioned to enlarge it. This extension comprised a new block with a tall spire. The church was reopened on 27 January 1870. The first minister of the congregation was the Rev. Dr David Landsborough (1779–1854), who was instrumental in having the church erected. He was a major figure in the burgh, having written the entry in the *New Statistical Account*, and he was noted as a botanist and geologist, particularly on the Island of Arran. During the outbreak of cholera in the town he did much to help his parishioners, but he contracted the disease and died of it. With the union of the U.F. Church and the Church of Scotland in 1929 this building was named the Landsborough Church. In 1968 the congregation was united with the Trinity Church, using the Trinity building. The Landsborough Church was demolished soon after.

SALTCOATS
NORTH CHURCH

Built in the gusset of Hamilton and Manse streets, the North Church was originally the Gaelic church. It was erected in 1836 by subscription, and according to the *New Statistical Account* was a 'neat small Gothic building, with Saxon door-way, small belfry – and the ground around it walled in, with pillars and iron rails in front.' It cost almost £1,000 and contained 720 seats. The building was fairly plain, but for the addition of spirelets at the corner of the eaves. The main entrance was located in the west gable, between stone-mullioned arched windows, and a small lancet high in the gable, below the dinky little belfry. Around the main doorway was a castellated stone surround. Built for the convenience of the local Gaelic speakers, it was in 1837 constituted a Gaelic Chapel by an Act of Assembly of the Church of Scotland. At the Disruption in 1843 the minister, the Rev. John Hamilton, left the Church of Scotland with most of his congregation, but they were allowed to remain in the church, calling themselves Saltcoats Free Gaelic Church, until the death of one of their ministers. In 1873 the number of Gaelic speakers in the district had

Saltcoats: North Church.

fallen to such an extent that the church was constituted as a Mission Church of the Church of Scotland, known as Saltcoats North. It attained quoad sacra status in 1906. In 1965 a new Saltcoats North Church was erected on the High Road, where numerous houses had been built in an ever-expanding town, and the old church was closed. The building was subsequently demolished and a supermarket now occupies the site.

SYMINGTON FREE CHURCH

The Free Church in Symington was established in 1843 when the Rev. George Orr left the parish church with many of his flock. At first they met in a former public house in the village, which was adapted to their needs. For a 'manse' the

Symington Free Church.

minister found lodgings in a hired room at a farm. Within a year a piece of ground at the Causey Foot was acquired and a new place of worship was erected. The building was a fairly plain Gothic structure, with Georgian glazed lancet windows. A small porch extended towards the street from the main gable, again with lancets and arched doorway. On the main gable, which had a thicker wall at the centre, was a shield bearing a date and a small belfry above. Below the eaves were carved barge boards. The Free Church was keen to have a Free Church School and manse in every parish, and the former school and manse at Symington survive, both now private houses. The manse had been erected in 1846 and was sold in 1932. It is a fine double-storey Georgian building. In 1848 the church had a membership of 210, falling to 64 in 1930, after the union with the Church of Scotland. The union had taken place on 30 November 1930.

CHAPTER 4

VILLAGES AND COMMUNITIES

ANNBANK STATION

The community of Annbank Station was established at the junction of the Ayr to Mauchline line with the Ayr to Edinburgh line. It was founded with the establishment of local mines by William Baird & Co. in 1897. Most of the houses dated from that time, but others were added in 1899. By 1913 there were 179 houses in the community, all of which were built of brick. Most of these came from the nearby Annbank brickworks, which operated for many years. As far as miners' homes were concerned, these rows were of a higher quality than most, having concrete pathways in front of them, gardens and drying greens. Most houses had wooden floors, and when James Brown inspected the village

Mossblown Top Row at Annbank Station.

in 1913 he noted that 'Mossblown is a decided improvement on many of the villages in the county.' For many years the village here had to suffer a double identity, being known variously as Mossblown or Annbank Station. Indeed a third name, Drumley, was also used to describe the small community of 36 two-apartment houses near to the Mauchline road. This was built around 1898 by George Taylor & Co., proprietors of Ayr Colliery. The railway station was known as Annbank Station, even although Annbank village was 1½ miles to the south. Similarly the public buildings such as the school and church originally took the Annbank name. It was only in recent years that it was decided that the village, which in the main now comprises twentieth-century council housing, should officially be known as Mossblown. Despite the loss of the old mines, the bings of which have been landscaped such that little sign of mining survives, the village has thrived, becoming a popular commuter village for Ayr, and new private housing has been added in recent years.

BENQUHAT

The Ordnance Survey and the Post Office insisted on calling the village Benquhat, but locals seemed to prefer the simpler spelling of Benwhat, which is how it was pronounced. The village comprised of five rows of miners' houses, perched high on the moor to the north of Dalmellington. The rows were around 1,050 feet above sea level, and were laid along the southern slopes of 1,427-foot high Benquhat Hill, from which they gained their name. The Dalmellington Iron Company built the houses for the miners employed in its iron pits, which went by the name of Corbie Craigs. Corbie Craigs was in fact

Benquhat village, showing the school to the left and store to the right.

another single row of ten houses, lower down the hillside at 850 feet. The first houses at Benquhat, known as the Laight Row, were erected in the early 1860s. This comprised twenty houses in a single terrace (to save the cost of erecting gables), each of which had a single room twenty feet by twelve feet doubling as a kitchen, with a small scullery of nine feet by eight feet to the rear. Built of the locally-made Dunaskin brick, latterly two houses were converted into a small miners' institute. Between 1870 and 1874 a further hundred and ten houses were erected in four rows to the rear of the first row. Each of the houses was much the same size as those in the first row, the only real difference being that the westmost row of twenty-eight houses was built of Dunaskin stone, the remainder of brick. The population in 1881 was 772. Benquhat had an old school from around 1865 until 1926, when a new school was opened. The old school, which was a stone building, was then converted into a village hall. There was also a co-operative store and beer-store, located in the same building. Electricity arrived in the village in 1933. Benquhat was abandoned in 1951 when the 460 residents were rehoused in Bellsbank and Dalmellington. The foundations of the rows remained for a time, but opencast workings have finally removed these, and today only the war memorial survives on the slopes of Benquhat Hill.

BURNFOOT & BURNSIDE

The village of Burnfoot and Burnside was located by the side of the New Cumnock to Dalmellington road, 2½ miles from New Cumnock. The oldest houses, seen in the foreground of the photograph, were the four rows that made

The Burnfoot Rows in the foreground with the later Burnside houses behind.

up Burnfoot Row. These comprised a total of forty-two houses and were built by Lanemark Coal Company, before being taken over by New Cumnock Collieries Ltd. In 1913 there were 234 people living in the rows, in very squalid conditions. Facilities in the village were poor, there being no wash houses, no coal houses, and only six earth closets with no doors to satisfy all the residents. Behind the right-hand row, which had two-apartment houses with sculleries, was the local football ground. The houses in the old rows were all condemned, and new houses were built immediately to the east, nearer to Burnfoot farm. This community, which is seen behind the rows, comprised eighty-six new houses, each with their own toilets, bathrooms and gardens. The chimneys beyond belonged to the Bank Colliery. In time the residents of the Burnside village gradually dwindled away as the local mines were closed. Over the years various blocks of houses were removed, until it too is now a distant memory, the last occupants being housed in new homes built at the Castle in New Cumnock.

COMMONDYKE

Commondyke is one of many lost villages that existed on the moors of eastern Ayrshire. It was located a mile and a half east of Auchinleck, on the farm of Commondyke, which predates the community and is the only building to survive. At one time there were a number of different miners' rows here, a co-operative store, railway station, football team and Roman Catholic church, school and convent. The village was established sometime in the late 1840s, when the Common coal pits were sunk. By 1878 there were 332 inhabitants in the sixty-five homes. The row illustrated was the Stable Row, seen here with its thatched roofs. This had six two-apartment and one single-apartment houses in it, and was at one time known as the Common Row. Owned by the trustees of Sir Claud Alexander of Ballochmyle, the houses were home to thirty-seven residents, who paid a rent of £5 per annum. They had to make do with a single wooden closet, and had neither ashpits nor wash houses. The sewage ran from the houses to the nearby burn. In 1867 the Birnieknowe Chapel was opened, followed by the school in 1878 and the convent in 1885. A sandstone cross in the field opposite where the chapel stood marks were a nun, Rev. Sister Laurienne Cusack, was killed by a train in 1888. She had been suffering from an infection that affected her hearing and was not aware of the train making its way along the siding. The village boasted a football team, known as Commondyke Celtic, which played on a field levelled out behind the

Commondyke: the old Stable Row.

coal bing from the houses. When the housing inspectors visited in 1913 they found a dismal sight; '. . . the stench is abominable . . . this is a horrible place.' A start on rehousing the residents was made before the Second World War, but this was held up during the years of hostilities. Over time the rows were pulled down and today only slight foundations on the ground mark where a large community once thrived.

CONNEL PARK

Connel Park was a sizeable mining community located one mile south west of New Cumnock. Built on the lands of South Boig farm, the village was originally erected in the 1870s to house workers and managers employed by the Nithsdale Iron Company, but when this venture failed ownership passed to the mine owners. The older houses were of stone, but later buildings were erected in brick. Thus Connel Park comprised of a number of miners' rows, homes for employees in the Knockshinnoch Castle Colliery and other pits. Others were employed in the local ironworks, and one row of houses had the name 'The Furnaces'. Unlike many mining communities, Connel Park's rows were not laid out back to back, but along both sides of streets, creating a more urban feel to the village. The names of the rows, however, were unimaginative, such as the Long Row, Store Row, Railway Terrace or New Football Row, named after the new football pitch. Connel Park even had a village centre, located at the cross

Top. Connel Park, near New Cumnock.
Above. Craigbank, near New Cumnock.

roads, where there was a branch of the co-op. Other commercial premises existed in the village, such as Murray the grocer. The village had a Baptist Church, but when the rows were demolished a new church was erected in New Cumnock in 1965–66 and the church came down soon after. Most of Connel Park has been cleared away, leaving only a few buildings. In recent years a large coal preparation plant has been created, transferring coal dug in local opencast mines onto the railway.

CRAIGBANK

The mining community of Craigbank was another of a series of villages strung out along the New Cumnock to Dalmellington road. Basically made up of five rows of houses, the village was more distinguished than some of the other communities as it had a public house (the two and a half storey building seen on the right of the picture) and a village store (further right), operated for many years by Gavin Lawrie and latterly known as Craigbank Stores. On the left are the eight houses that formed the first section of Front Row, and behind it can be seen the roofs and chimneys of Plantation Row. Miners living here were employed in the main at the Lanemarks Collieries or else the Bank Collieries and Brickworks. Craigbank was originally owned by the Hyslops of Bank, followed by New Cumnock Collieries Ltd. In 1913 the village had a population of 247, and even as late as that time there was a lack of facilities. According to 'Evidence Submitted to the Royal Commission of Housing' in 1913 by James Brown of the Ayrshire Miners' Union, 'how the people who are condemned to live here manage to exist is a mystery. It is alleged that one lady visitor lately had to go out into the open moss, no other accommodation being available. She is not likely to repeat the experience.' At that time he was delighted to report that new homes were in the course of erection, 'of a superior character', complete with bathroom, water-closet, scullery and coal bunker in the house. When these houses, known as The Crescent, were completed, Peesweep Row, Stable Row and part of Blair Street, were demolished. Today there are no buildings at all left in Craigbank.

CRAIGMARK

Craigmark was an old mining village located to the north of Dalmellington. Established by the Dalmellington Iron Company, there were seventy-three houses in total, fifty-two of which had two apartments, and twenty-one of which were single apartments. The houses were built around 1840 of stone, but were rather small. Indeed, one of the houses had a kitchen measuring fourteen feet by eight feet, and a room of similar sizes. In this house lived eleven people! The kitchens had two inset iron beds in them. There were also rows in the village known as Dublin rows, sometimes erroneously thought to derive from the high number of Irish-born residents, but deriving from the fact that these houses were formed from two joined together, or 'double-end'. Each of the houses had a water-closet and coal-house and every four tenants shared a wash-house. The sewage arrangements were negligible, comprising only of a settling tank that was never cleaned and which was extremely foul in warm weather. Craigmark had a co-operative store, village school, smithy and public house. The population in 1861 was 543, peaking at 616 in 1881. The village was cleared away when new houses of a better standard were erected at nearby Burnton. The first of these houses were built in 1924, and by the 1930s, when the residents were rehoused, the old rows were demolished. At Burnton, when the new junior football team was founded in 1929, it was given the name Craigmark Burntonians, commemorating the old village. It is now based in Dalmellington. At Craigmark only the former pub survives, serving an ever-dwindling clientele

CRONBERRY

Some of the former mining village of Cronberry still survives. A row of 1920s houses, which were built when there was still a demand for homes in such a rural location, still exists, perched on the edge of Airds Moss, alongside the Bello Water. Beyond these can still be made out the foundations of the original village, which comprised seven rows of homes. Cronberry was built in 1862 to house miners employed in the coal and ironstone mines that were located on the moors hereabouts. The houses were owned by the local coal and ironstone miners, William Baird & Co. Conditions in the old rows were particularly poor. For example, the first row, which had eight homes, was home to 101 people. The houses had no fires other than in the kitchen, and they were particularly damp. Other rooms had similar problems, and for 600 residents there was not one washing-house, no paved ways outside the houses, and all the windows were fastened closed. The seventh row was the finest, and gained the name Store Row from the fact that the co-op had a branch here. This row was where the better off residents lived, such as the schoolmaster, policeman and various

Top. Craigmark rows, near Dalmellington.
Above. Cronberry Store Row.

Top. Darnconner, showing its last resident about to leave.
Above. Gadgirth Holm cottages.

foremen. This row was made from stone and had slate roofs, whereas the other rows were of brick, and three of these had tarred felt roofs. These 'Tarry Rows' were first to be emptied and were demolished by 1925. The remainder of the houses were gradually emptied and the residents rehoused in Logan, outside Cumnock. The rows were eventually demolished by the mid 1960s.

DARNCONNER

The village of Darnconner was located in the parish of Auchinleck, two miles north east of Auchinleck itself. Remotely located on Airds Moss, the village became quite independent, and had most of its own facilities. These included a parish church (which is depicted in the previous chapter) and co-operative store, which included a bakery. One of the houses was the home of a policeman. Sometime between 1860–69 the Eglinton Iron Company erected a school here, which was transferred to the school board in 1887. A new school house (one of only two buildings that survive of the village) was erected in 1899. Darnconner was established in the 1850s, following the sinking of various Common Coal Pits. Originally the village comprised six rows of houses, totalling thirty-four, formed into two open squares, the Low Square and High Square. Added to these were the Railway Rows, School Row and Store Row. Sometime prior to 1900 the Commonloch Row was built, a long row of 96 houses, built end to end round a dog-leg. These houses were built adjoining each other to save on the cost of building gables. In 1878 the village had a population of 554. After the First World War many of the older houses had become uninhabitable, and many residents were rehoused in new council homes in Auchinleck. By 1932 only twenty-seven families remained at Darnconner, the co-op having closed in 1931. The school and church were both closed in 1939. The photograph shows Archie Stewart, the last resident of the rows prior to him leaving the village for good.

GADGIRTH HOLM

At one time there were numerous tiny hamlets all over the county, occupied by workers who were employed in small-scale local mines, mills, or estates. Gadgirth Holm was one of these, located by the side of the River Ayr, on the south side of Gadgirth Bridge, in the parish of Coylton. Gadgirth estate was anciently a seat of the Chalmers family, and Mary Queen of Scots and John

Knox were visitors. The ancient castle, which was perched on a high promontory overlooking the River Ayr, was in 1808 replaced by a Georgian mansion, perhaps by the same architect as Logan House near Cumnock. Later owners were the Kennedys, Burnetts, and Ayr County Council, who ran the house as a children's home. The house was demolished in 1968. In 1841 the population of Gadgirth Holm was estimated at fifty and most were employed in local mines. One of the residents was Samuel MacCutcheon, noted for telling lies. He once claimed to have seen an eel that had its tail wrapped three times round the Gadgirth Bridge, and its head up at Stair, worrying sheep! The old row of cottages was demolished in the early part of the twentieth century and replaced with a new terrace of cottages in 1906.

GASSWATER

Nothing of Gasswater village survives today, other than a few overgrown hawthorn bushes that formerly marked the boundaries of the village gardens. The community comprised four rows of houses and was strung out along the road between Cumnock and Muirkirk, four miles from the former. The village was created by William Baird & Co., which owned the ironworks at Lugar. The houses predate 1860, when the rows were known as Brick Row, Stone Row, Baxter's Row and School Row. The School Row was named after the school, which seems only to have existed for a short time, probably replaced by that at

Gasswater cottages.

Cronberry, when that community was founded in 1862. In 1859 the teacher at Gasswater was John Cooper. Two of the rows were made of stone cottages, the others of brick. When an inspector for the Royal Commission on Housing visited in 1913 he found the village becoming abandoned, the homes too far decayed for occupancy. Of the forty houses in the community, eleven were empty, and the other homes had a population of 97. The inspector described the rows as having 'no wash-houses, no coalhouses, and there is one closet without doors for the twelve houses' in row number four. Stable Row was abandoned by 1910, by 1920 half of the houses were empty, and in 1930 only three houses in Baxter's Row were still occupied.

GLENBUCK

At one time Ayrshire's most easterly village, Glenbuck has a history that seems to be greater than the size of the village would merit. The first signs of development in the area occurred in 1760 when the New Mills Weaving Company established a branch here. In 1802 the mossy hollow below Hareshaw Hill was dammed at either end to create Glenbuck Loch. This was needed to supply water to Catrine Cotton Mills, which were located on the River Ayr, seventeen miles downstream. Early in the morning the dam sluices would be opened and the waters would flow down the River Ayr to the mill wheel, by which time the factory was ready to start work. In 1790 some English

Glenbuck's main street.

entrepreneurs established Glenbuck Iron Works, but these were fairly unsuccessful, and went out of business. However, the mining for coal associated with the works was a success, and the extraction of coal continues until present times. A number of miners' rows were laid out alongside the Stottencleugh Burn, and at one time the village had a population of 1,750. To meet the needs of the residents there was a church, erected in 1881, a school erected in 1876, a branch of Muirkirk Ironworks Co-operative Society (closed in 1953), a timber public hall (opened in September 1904 by J.G.A. Baird MP and burned down after its closing meeting in October 1953) and a railway station. The village was known for its top quoits players, but more importantly for its football team. Glenbuck Cherrypickers was established in the 1870s and played until 1932. Its unusual name would have probably been enough to ensure its place in history, but a son of the village and former player ensured this. Bill Shankly was born here in 1913 and went on to become the manager of Liverpool FC, one of the most successful football managers there has ever been. After he died in 1981 a memorial was erected at Glenbuck to commemorate him. Today Glenbuck is possibly going to be revived in a new guise, as a crofting community. Blocks of land with a house and steading are being created, reviving a long-lost village.

GLENBURN

The village of Glenburn was established on the edge of Prestwick in 1911 by Auchincruive Coal Co., a division of Bairds. Three rows of double-storey

Glenburn, near Prestwick.

tenement buildings were erected of Sanquhar brick to house miners employed in the Glenburn pit, or Auchincruive 4/5, as it was officially known. This employed up to 700 men, most of whom lived in the adjoining rows, totalling 187 homes. Unlike many miners' homes, which were built as cheaply as possible, Glenburn hinted at some form of architectural influence, with small dormer gables added to break up the line of what would be a long frontage of brick. The village was a higher class of mining community, each home having a sizeable garden to front and rear, which allowed the residents to grow vegetables. In addition, water, gas and sewerage were provided. In the middle of the community, in a central square, was the public wash house, or 'steamie', where the weekly wash could be carried out. When built, Glenburn was regarded as a 'model village' for the housing of miners, even although the owners did not go as far as supplying each house with its own toilet or bath. Electricty did not arrive until after nationalisation of the mining industry in 1947. A village school was opened on 25 October 1915, designed by William Cowie, having 305 pupils by 1919. The village was abandoned in the 1960s, and was demolished between 1969 and 71. It has been noted that the cost of pulling the houses down was £50, £10 more than it cost to build them! Glenburn Pit itself was closed in 1973. The site of the village is now occupied by modern housing in Blackford Crescent and Langcroft Avenue. Glenburn School survives, much expanded and still serving the local community.

HIGHHOUSE ROWS – AUCHINLECK

The miners' rows at Highhouse Colliery, just to the west of Auchinleck, were erected to house men who worked in the pit. William Baird & Company sank Highhouse in 1894 and they added 96 houses to the west of the mine, alongside the Barony Road. This road was referred to as the 'Via Sacra' in James Boswell's journals, and the Boswells were so influential in the parish that they managed to have the houses built with their back to the main road, to prevent the miners from standing at their doors watching the Boswells as they made their way to the church. There were two rows, of forty-nine and forty-eight houses, each of two apartments, the rent of which was two shillings and a penny per week in 1913. Inside there was a kitchen of thirteen feet by eleven feet, the room of twelve feet by ten feet, and both of these were floored with timber. The kitchens had an oven grate. The row adjoining the Barony Road was built of stone, the rear row made from brick, but otherwise similar in size. Four houses shared a wash house and closet. The Highhouse Rows were

Top. The rows at Highhouse, on the edge of Auchinleck.
Above. Kames, near Muirkirk, with the Ironworks cottages to the right,
and the start of Linkieburn Square to the left.

demolished in February 1959, the residents having been given new houses elsewhere in Auchinleck. A second group of rows in the village, Dalsalloch Rows, were likewise demolished in April 1964. A fragment of some of the Highhouse buildings was to survive, and remains as part of the small industrial estate that was established on the site.

KAMES

Known to folk in Muirkirk as the 'South Side' the official name for the former mining community was Kames, sometime spelled 'Kaimes'. The illustration shows what was known as the Ironworks Cottages, which still survive, and the Linkyburn Square rows to their left. The ornate gateposts mark the entrance to the Kames institute, erected in 1903–04, latterly used as an outdoor centre. There were at least six other rows at Kames, though none had homes so fine as those illustrated here. Also at Kames was Muirkirk railway station. In 1913 the village had 237 houses within it, and the population was 1,064. This figure was rather low, as it was noted that Linkyburn Square 'is tenanted by Spaniards, making it a little difficult to get exact figures'. These houses were fourteen feet by twelve feet and were built of stone. Beyond the church was Midhouse Row, comprising twenty-five houses in a single row, supplied with five washing-houses and a dry-closet per three homes. Two rows were named Railway Terrace, with twenty-six and twenty-seven houses respectively, and were built of stone. To the west were three brick rows, named Kames Row. The residents of the village were classed as being quite decent folk, for they had gardens in which they grew vegetables, and the plentiful supply of clean water from Cairn Table meant that the community was reasonably clean. The inspectors who visited in 1913 stated that, 'On the whole this is a good type of village. A very little trouble and expense would make it a desirable place to live in.' However, as the years passed by and the mines were closed, the residents of Kames began to leave. Most were rehoused in the new council houses at Smallburn, just west of Muirkirk, which were built from 1930–50.

KERSE

Kerse was a small mining community located by the side of the Smithston Burn, in the parish of Dalrymple. Sometimes known as Kerse Square, the community was founded to house miners employed in the local ironstone pits, which were latterly owned by the Dalmellington Iron Company. There were only twenty houses at Kerse, located on the north side of Smithston Upper Bridge, which appears in the foreground of the picture. The sign at the eaves of the building in the picture indicates the village store, where the residents could purchase their provisions. The building in the trees was the village school, provided by Dalrymple School Board. This building was later to be condemned by the Inspectorate for being damp, and overrun by rats, which were wont to eat the children's lunches. A new school was erected further up the road in 1914, to plans by Ayr architect, Alexander Caldwell Thomson (d. 1925), serving both Kerse and Cairntable. The houses at Kerse were removed in the mid 1920s when the residents were rehoused at Polnessan, a row of double-storey cottages built by Ayr County Council alongside the main Doon valley road.

LETHANHILL

Lethanhill, or 'The Hill' as the locals of the Doon valley knew it, actually comprised two villages, Burnfoothill and Lethanhill. These were located close to each other on the high plateau of Knockkippen Hill, on the east side of the Doon valley. Lethanhill was the larger of the two communities, and it had the few facilities that were offered to the miners who lived in the rows. Originally there was no road into the village, the residents being expected to walk the incline down to Burnfoot. At a later date a rough road was created climbing the hill from Patna. Lethanhill was one of the highest villages in Ayrshire, being located well over 900 feet above sea level. The Ordnance Survey benchmark on the school building was 960 feet above the sea. Twelve rows of houses made up Lethanhill, the Low Row being depicted here. There were three rows of houses that made up the Low Row, stretching alongside a mineral railway, and totalling sixty-five houses. The Old School Row had twenty-four houses, the Briggate Row twenty houses, and the White Brick Row twenty-one houses. The Stone Row was named from having been erected of stone, and had sixteen houses. The Whaup Row comprised fifteen houses, the Store Row only four houses, and the same number in the Diamond Row. The Step Row had twenty houses, though at one time it had more. Burnfoothill had three rows in a line, totalling sixty-nine houses. Many of the larger figures were a bit fluid, for in many cases, to create larger homes, two houses were knocked into one. The oldest rows at Lethanhill date from the late 1840s, and were built to house miners employed in the Bowhill and Drumgrange pits. At its peak, Lethanhill had 1,690 residents, living in a total of around 300 houses. Lethanhill had a

Top. Kerse Square, with the village store in the centre and old school in the trees.
Above. Lethanhill.

branch store of the Dalmellington Iron Company, a new school building of around 1875, extended in 1912, and replaced by a third school in 1928. There was also a mission hall, or church. The latter was erected of timber and corrugated iron in 1904, at a cost of £299, but it was later to be adorned with a simple brick-built belfry. The residents of Lethanhill were gradually rehoused in Patna after the Second World War, though the first residents to move in 1947 were rather reluctant to leave. The last resident to move out did so in 1954 and the old rows were gradually demolished. The church was dismantled and taken to Dalmellington, where it served as the silver band hall for many years. Foundations of some of the buildings remain, now mainly lost in a pine plantation.

LUGAR ROWS

The village of Lugar lies to the east of Cumnock, by the side of the Lugar Water. It was established in 1845 to house workers employed in Lugar ironworks, and also colliers and ironstone miners who dug the raw materials from the ground. Today the village survives as an elongated community, mainly comprising late miners' rows (Park Terrace, built in 1928) and council houses. When built, Lugar had a number of typical miners' rows in it, the Craigstonholm Row of twenty-seven houses, Store Row of seven houses, Back Row with fifteen houses, Belloholm Row (twenty-four houses in two blocks) and the Peesweep Rows (twenty-three houses in two rows). To this were added the Back Row (seventy-seven houses) and the Crescent, of twenty-seven houses. Many of the houses were built of blonde sandstone, but some were brick-built. The village had its own church (which survives), co-operative store, school and institute. A house in Belloholm Row doubled as a police station. The picture shows the Belloholm and Front Rows, lining the main road to Muirkirk, with the Back (or Brick) Row behind. The tall chimneys on the hill-top belong to the ironworks, and the smaller chimney behind the Back Row was associated with the gas works. Lugar's maximum population was 1,850, reached in 1908. Lugar ironworks were closed in November 1928 and Lugar Pit in 1954. The old rows were demolished, the occupants being given new homes in the nearby community of Logan, established on a greenfield site on the opposite side of the river. Craigstonholm Row went first, demolished in 1958, and the Front and Brick rows followed in 1961. The site of the old rows has in most places been rebuilt with newer houses, though the houses at the top of the Peesweep Brae and the Crescent are occupied by forestry.

*Lugar village, with the ironworks on the hill,
and the workers' cottages below.*

SPRINGSIDE – BANK END

The village of Springside as it is today is an amalgam of small mining communities, most of which has been rebuilt over the years. The original Springside comprised of the three Kirkland Rows and Springside Square, and was located north of the railway line, at Springside Farm. South of the railway line was the village of Bankhead, and to the west of this were the Springhill and Corsehill rows. All the names were very much interchangeable, for Springhill Institute was located at Bankhead. In 1913 conditions in the rows, which were mainly owned by A. Finnie & Sons or A. Kenneth & Sons, was dire. There were reports of part of Springside Square falling into ruin, and in the 'Six Rows' the walls were damp and some were unplastered. This old postcard depicts Bank End, which was the eastern part of Bankhead, and shows old cottages alongside what was the main road between Irvine and Kilmarnock. The cottages shown were a better quality than the common miner was supplied with, for these had sizeable gardens around them, and a water pump can be seen in the street. The pit behind was Springhill Colliery (Pit Number 2), which was operated by J. & R. Howie Ltd. There were four different shafts sunk in the area, but Springhill Colliery was abandoned in 1927.

Top. Bank End, Springside.
Above. Tongue Bridge Row.

TONGUE BRIDGE ROW

The Tongue Bridge Row, or Tongue Row as it was also known, was one of many little mining communities that were dotted all over the Ayrshire coalfield. The row of stone-built houses was located in the parish of Dalrymple, between Patna and Littlemill. Built by the local mineowners, most of the residents were employed in the Bowhill and Kerse ironstone pits, which littered the high moor hereabouts. When built, the row comprised forty houses, but over the years sometimes two adjoining houses were knocked into one, to make a more commodious house. The row was later acquired by the Dalmellington Iron Company and it was probably after this that the village store, known as Kerse Store, a branch of the company store at Waterside, was opened in one of the buildings. Houses numbered 22 and 23 were at one time converted into a small mission hall, where religious services could be held. A school was erected nearby at Kerse in 1914 which served the local mining communities until 1962. As part of its scheme for rehousing the occupants of old and decaying miners' rows, Ayr County Council erected new homes at nearby Polnessan and the row was abandoned and demolished in the 1930s.

WESTON ROW – ANNBANK

Annbank village was established in the 1860s by George Taylor & Co., which was a mining company based in the Ayr district. They had the mining rights to the Auchincruive and Enterkine estates, and established a number of pits in the area. The coal was taken to Ayr, often by a small railway, where it was either sold locally or exported from the harbour. On the first Ordnance Survey map of 1860 no village of Annbank is shown, but at Weston farm was a smithy and a small school, serving the local community. The houses were built soon after this, forming an elongated village alongside the road between Weston Smiddy and the gates to Annbank House. Most of the houses were single apartment homes, but the mining company had gradually added additional rooms to these, making them more comfortable. A supply of fresh water was available from Loch Bradan, but there was also a village pump drawing local hard water, which some of the residents preferred. In the village were a post office, a corrugated-iron chapel of ease, erected in 1871, a store, a reading room and a school. The church was replaced by a new place of worship in 1903, when the present building was erected at nearby Annbank Station (now known as Mossblown), designed by John B. Wilson, and the school, presently known as

Weston Row at Annbank.

Mossblown Primary School, in the same year, the work of John Eaglesham. One of the residents of Annbank was James Brown (1862–1939), who became a prominent MP, Privy Councillor, and three times Lord High Commissioner to the Church of Scotland. He was instrumental in getting improvements for the village, and is commemorated by a memorial in the village square. Most of the old rows were demolished in the 1930s and 1940s, to be replaced by more modern council housing. Today there is little to hint that Annbank was once a mining community.

CHAPTER 5
TOWN HOUSES, TENEMENTS AND SHOPS

✳

ARDROSSAN
EGLINTON ARMS HOTEL

Erected in 1806–07, the Eglinton Arms was one of the original buildings of the new town of Ardrossan that was established at the harbour by Hugh, 12th Earl of Eglinton. He had built a new port and adjoining town in the early years of the nineteenth century, using the architect Peter Nicholson of Glasgow to furnish a plan. This comprised a gridded town, made up mainly of Glasgow and Montgomerie streets, with a fine crescent of mansions overlooking South

The Eglinton Arms Hotel in Ardrossan.

Bay. Although the proposed canal linking the town with Glasgow was never completed, Ardrossan flourished. The Eglinton Arms was built as the major coaching inn of his new town, and it offered a high standard of service. According to the *New Statistical Account*, written in 1837, the hotel was 'one of the best in any country town in Scotland [and] affords every accommodation which can be required. It contains ten public rooms, and eighteen bed-rooms, with cold and warm baths.' The Earl used the hotel for guests staying in the locality. To the rear were extensive stables, latterly converted into a garage. The architect of the building was also Nicholson, who created a fine, if fairly plain, classical house, which was erected at a cost of £10,000. Symmetrical from the front, the main block was five bays in width on the ground and first floors, the second floor only being three bays wide. Simple pilasters framed the outermost bays, and the main entrance was through a simple classic porch with curved corners. To the west side of the main block was a flanking pavilion, added sometime in the late nineteenth century. The Eglinton Arms Hotel was burned down in the 1990s and subsequently demolished.

AYR
BACK O' THE ISLE

This little street in Ayr is known officially as Hope Street, which it has been since around 1850, but previously it was the Isle Lane, or just the Isle, and even today folk still refer to it as the Back o' the Isle. The Isle referred to are the blocks of buildings which occupy the site of the old tolbooth of Ayr. Hope Street is a rather narrow lane to be styled 'street', but it is still a popular route for shoppers making their way along the High Street, preferring to take this route rather than around the outer side of the Isle. The sketch shown here was made in 1887 by Robert Bryden, but even he at that time noted that the overhanging balcony had been removed. This was probably one of the last of such in Ayr, and had existed from the time when building out into the street at first floor or higher level was quite normal. In some places the area below the balcony was built in, but in this case the whole building was to be removed. This building, with the round tower adjoining, was at one time part of the town house of the Kennedys of Cassillis. The Kennedys were renowned for feuding, both with other clans and with branches within the same family, and this house seems to have been designed as a place where they could hide if need be. The house had a large fireplace within it, with a wide ingle, and should the occupiers of the house come under attack they were able to enter the fireplace and climb up

Left. A view down Hope Street, or the 'Back o' the Isle', Ayr.
Right. Blair's House in Ayr.

steps within the chimney for around ten feet to a secret chamber. It was in Hope Street that Count Hamilton, the author of *Memoirs of Grammont*, is said to have been born. The street retains some of its old-world character, with smaller shop premises here than in the rest of the High Street, but most of the buildings have been reconstructed since this sketch was made.

AYR
BLAIR'S HOUSE

This ancient building was located off Ayr High Street, and today is covered by the large shop occupied by Marks & Spencer, erected in 1972 to plans by James M. Munro & Partners of Glasgow. The house had a variety of names over its life, being known variously as Blair's House, Gadgirth House, or MacKill's Close. The original building is thought to have been erected sometime before 1470, the earliest reference there is to it, when it was mentioend as the 'new tenement' of John Blair of Adamton. Many Ayrshire gentry had town houses in the county town, either for business, or else for living in during the winter months, when remote castles were too cold for their liking. The house was to pass into the ownership of another Ayrshire landowning family, the Chalmers of Gadgirth. They sold it in 1654 to Thomas Blair, merchant in the town and a cadet of Adamton. The town house was originally quite a large building, extending to the High Street, where a large turreted block existed. This was said to have been the lodging house of John Mair, a noted grammarian and author of *Introduction to Latin Syntax*, who became Rector of Ayr Academy. That part was latterly removed when new buildings were erected on the High Street. Blair's Tenement occupied three main blocks, joined at right angles to each other. The west block was separated from the east range at ground floor level by the passage seen in the left of the sketch (p. 127). An external stairway to the east of this, shown in the sketch, led to the first floor, originally reached through the doorway seen to the left of the landing. This led to the stair tower, which was located within the corbie-stepped gable to the left, and which contained a turnpike stairway. Externally this tower was adorned with carved panels, no doubt containing arms. The main floor contained a hall and various other rooms, and over it were a number of chambers and attic rooms. In later years the house was converted into a furniture sale room, occupied by one MacKill, who also ran a pawnbroking business, and later again was converted into a bakehouse, at which time some of it was rebuilt. The house was demolished in the spring of 1972, but a survey of the building was carried out at that time. It was the third-last medieval town house to survive in Ayr, the last two, Loudoun Hall and Lady Cathcart's House, having been rescued and restored.

AYR
MARY BOYD'S CLOSE

Mary Boyd's Close was one of many little lanes and alleyways that led off the principal thoroughfares of Ayr's central main streets. This close left what is now Hope Street, and extended into the back riggs of the properties that faced onto High Street. The development of Scots burghs often followed the model of feus being allocated along the principal street of the burgh, in Ayr's case originally Sandgate, but latterly High Street was developed in the same way. These feus had short frontages onto the main street, but they extended many yards backwards, giving the occupier a considerable garden area. As towns developed, many of these 'back riggs' were built on, dwellings and business premises being added in a linear fashion. Access to such riggs was by way of

Mary Boyd's Close in Ayr.

narrow lanes or pends, leading from the main street, and often there was no linking access between them. Few of these lanes survive in Ayr, but some can be seen off the west side of New Bridge Street, or to the rear of the Tam o' Shanter Inn. Mary Boyd's Close was accessed from a doorway adjacent to the Kennedy of Cassillis' town house. Who Mary Boyd was is not known. Part of the building in the close was erected in 1583, as noted on an armorial datestone over one of the doorways. The arms incorporate three lozenges and three stars, probably indicating the Mure family. The doorway itself, which had a fine carved roll moulding around it, had the initials 'IP' and 'SK' carved into the lintel, the 'K' no doubt for one of the Kennedys. Robert Bryden drew this sketch in 1887, but even then the lane was being redeveloped, and the old carved stones were destroyed. Many other old Scots burghs tended to preserve their old stones and incorporate them in the buildings that were to be built on the same site, but most, if not all, Ayrshire towns did not follow this tradition, preferring to get rid of the old and replace it with new work.

Top. John Murdoch's House in Ayr Sandgate,
where Robert Burns received part of his education.
Above. The town house of the Neill's of Swindridgemuir in Ayr.

AYR
MURDOCH'S HOUSE

This typical Scots burgh dwelling at 58 Sandgate, Ayr, would not have gathered much notice in its lifetime if it were not for the fact that it was the home of John Murdoch. He was the burgh schoolmaster from 1772–76 and in 1773 one of his young charges was none other than Robert Burns, who later was to become famous as a poet. The bard's father sent him to lodge with Murdoch for three weeks, during which time he was to improve his English grammar and to receive lessons in French. The house was typical of many in the Sandgate at that time, built of random rubble and roofed with thatch. To the rear were additions down the burgage plot, often sub-let to poorer families. The sketch is not too accurate in its representation of the building, for a photograph exists which shows a fourth, smaller window to the right of the door. Murdoch's house was demolished in 1894 and a shop erected on the site, to the plans of H.V. Eaglesham. On the gable of the present building a plaque commemorates Burns' connection with the site. This reads, *Here stood the house of John Murdoch, schoolmaster, in which Robert Burns lodged in his 14th year and received lessons in English and French.* In 1776 John Murdoch, under the influence of drink, criticised the local minister, the Rev. William Dalrymple, and was obliged to leave the burgh. He headed for London, where he remained until his death in 1824.

AYR
NEILL'S HOUSE

The town house of the Neills of Swindridgemuir was located in what was latterly known as Terry's Close, off Ayr High Street. This was located at 26–30 High Street but was demolished in 1914 when the foundation stone of a new hall for the YMCA was laid. Designed by Stewart Kaye, an architect from Dunfermline, this building too has been removed, and modern shops now occupy the site. The Neills were a long-established Ayrshire county family, their principal seat being Swindridgemuir House, which stands a couple of miles to the east of Dalry. They also owned Barnweill, in the parish of Craigie. The most prominent member of the family was no doubt General James George Smith Neill (1810–57), who was a hero of the Indian Mutiny at Cawnpore. He was born in the Neill's later town house, which was located in Wellington Square, but was shot at the relief of Lucknow on 25 September 1857. In 1859, to honour his military achievements, the people of Ayr erected a statue to him in Wellington Square, sculpted by Mathew Noble, and other memorials in India commemorate him. The name Terry's Close comes from James Terry & Son, who ran a locksmith and bell-hanging business from a building at the head of the lane.

AYR
SANDGATE HOUSE

Sandgate House stood at the southern end of Ayr's street of that name, on what was the southern extremity of the town. The house was erected around 1780 by John Boswell (1741–1805), Writer in Ayr. He was a cadet of the Auchinleck Boswell family, and was to be an ancestor of the Boswells who inherited Garrallan estate near Cumnock from the Douglases. The house was a typical Georgian building of its period, but which was extended a number of times. One of these extensions was the large double-storey entrance hall, complete with its own low-pitched roof, which had large square pillars supporting a small porch. The wing to the right, seen in the photograph as it was being demolished, was probably another addition, as was a similar wing to the left. In 1907 the grounds of Sandgate House were laid out to form two streets – Boswell Park and Douglas Street, names taken from the family. In 1936 the house was sold to the Post Office, but redevelopment was stifled by the outbreak of war. The house was subsequently demolished in 1952 and the present building, formerly the post office, was erected on the site.

AYR
SENIOR'S ORGAN SALOONS

The premises of Edward Senior were located at 141–143 High Street, a spot now incorporated in the former Littlewoods Store, the first half of which was built in 1968, and the second, which covered the ground where Senior's stood, following a number of years later. Edward Senior was a seller of all sorts of musical instruments, originally located elsewhere. However, in 1907 his business was so successful that he could afford to build a specially-designed 'pianoforte and organ saloon', rising over four floors plus an attic. The plans were produced by William MacClelland and dated 4 October 1907; within a year the new shop was opened for business. Such was the success that

Top. Sandgate House, Ayr, as it was being demolished.
Above. Senior's organ saloons in Ayr High Street.

additions to the rear had to be drawn up in 1908, again by MacLelland. MacLelland was one of those middling architects who never seem to have had the chance to make their mark on anything of significance. However, for Senior he was able to produce an attractively detailed shop, the lower two floors of which had large expanses of plate glass, illuminating the showrooms within, which was a 'noted house for violins, cellos, basses, mandolins [sic], guitars, banjos, etc'. The third and fourth floors were heavier as far as masonry was concerned, the windows being smaller. At eaves' level the stonework was carved with a flourish of patterns, balusters, pillars and the date. Over all rose a gable facing the street, again ornamented with a fine selection of classical carvings.

IRVINE
JOHN GALT'S HOUSE

The house in which the famous novelist John Galt (1779–1839) was born in Irvine's High Street was demolished in 1858 to allow the erection of a branch of the Union Bank of Scotland. This building has in turn been razed to the ground, and the site is now occupied by a modern Bank of Scotland, erected as part of Irvine's redevelopment as a New Town. A bronze plaque, sculpted by Robert Bryden, commemorates the novelist. Galt's birthplace was a typical Scots burgh tenement, comprising three floors and as many flats. The Galts are thought to have occupied the middle flat, access to which was made by walking through the close on the left of the ground floor and ascending a stairway to the rear of the building. According to the old title deeds of the building, this was a large tenement of land, complete with brewhouses, offices, backhouse and a yard. It was at Galt's birth the property of Margaret Dunlop – she was a daughter of Elizabeth Galt, so the Galt family were no doubt connected to her. Galt's house had a frontage of five bays, the lower flat being accessed from the street through a doorway. A pend passed through the southern end of the building. Standing upright, the building had a high pitched roof with crow-stepped gables. John Galt moved to Greenock at an early age, where he found employment as a customs officer. He later moved to London, where he became an agent for a company promoting emigration to Upper Canada. Galt himself left for the dominion, and founded the town of Guelph. His longing for Scotland led him to write novels based on traditional characters, and his *Ayrshire Legatees, The Entail,* and *The Annals of the Parish*, are still published as classic Scottish works to this day.

The house where novelist John Galt was born in Irvine.

IRVINE POLYTECHNIC

Irvine Polytechnic was located at 12 Bridgegate, on the north side of the street. John Colvin dealt in all sorts of hardware and fancy goods, and in the Irvine Directory of 1898 he is listed as selling drysalted goods, glass goods, hardware, ironmongery, seeds and toys, as well as being an insurance agent. His advertisement detailed much more that he sold, though the quality of poetry he used leaves much to be desired!

The polytechnic is the place
To get things up to date,
And prices are the very keenest,
With quality to compensate.

There's goblets, pots, and frying pans,
Bread, table, and pocket knives,
Cradles, washing boards, sure to please,
Men, maids and married wives.

And so on! Polytechnics were common throughout Scotland, being stores that sold a multitude of things, and Colvin's was no exception. His premises were quite small, for modern shops, but in its day the three floors of goods would be a veritable emporium to the shopper. The ground floor was faced with timber, surrounding large glass windows. At first- and second-floor level the rusticated masonry was visible, the voussoirs of the first-floor windows being painted to include 'The Polytechnic'. As with all of the north side of the Bridgegate, this building was demolished in the early 1970s to allow the erection of Bridgegate House, designed in 1973 by Irvine Development Corporation architects.

Irvine Polytechnic.

IRVINE
TIMMERLAND

The old building known as Timmerland stood in Irvine at the corner of Bridgegate with Main Street (later named High Street). It had no real historical significance, other than the fact that it was probably the last of many traditional burgh houses of its type. The building was in the main erected of stone, and roofed over with slates, but it had an extended frontage into the street, built of timber, hence the name of the building. This consisted of wooden pillars supporting a timber canopy. Encroachment of the public highway was often troublesome since it caused congestion, and most burghs passed local acts to deal with such situations. In many cases the projection was added to the original building at a later date, often to cover market stalls or booths that had gradually become semi-permanent. The veranda was also useful in preventing pedestrians from having to walk on the rough and dirty streets, the open drains of which were often filled with stagnant water. Timmerland also sported two small gables at roof level, known as nepus gables, which were a common feature in old Scots vernacular architecture. The premises of John Davidson, ironmonger in the town, are seen across the High Street at Number 90. It was later owned by James A. Davidson, but this building, too, has long gone. It was typical old Scots burgh vernacular, with crow steps and Georgian windows.

The Timmerland at Irvine Cross.

Top. Bank of Scotland in Kilmarnock's Portland Street.
Above. John Boyle's Shop in Kilmarnock.

KILMARNOCK
BANK OF SCOTLAND

One of a number of lost banking premises in Kilmarnock, this branch of the Bank of Scotland was located in Portland Street. A palazzo-style building, it was designed by James Ingram (1799–1879) and erected around 1850. In style it was very similar to the Union Bank in Ayr High Street, designed by Robert Paton, which is of a similar, if slightly wider, style, and which dates from 1856. Originally a branch of the British Linen Bank, this was taken over by the Bank of Scotland. Whereas the Ayr bank had six bays of windows, the Kilmarnock bank was only five bays in width. The ground floor was fronted with a white granite façade, completed with fluted columns. Two doorways gave access to the building, that to the left to the bank chambers on the upper floors, the one on the right to the banking hall. At first floor level the windows were fairly plain, only the centre one having a small pediment over it (compare Ayr, where the six windows are pedimented), and the second floor windows were plain. Like Ayr there was a decorative balustrade at eaves' level. With the redevelopment of Portland Street, most of the buildings around the bank were cleared away, being of an older date and not so well built, leaving the bank, which had closed business as such, standing in isolation. Campaigns to save the building were fruitless, and eventually it too was pulled down and replaced by the present steel-framed and concrete block-infill shops.

KILMARNOCK
JOHN BOYLE'S SHOP

The shop belonging to John Boyle at 123–127 King Street in Kilmarnock was a fine renaissance structure, divided into two premises on the ground floor. The upper floor was all Boyle's. Originally the building on this site contained three shops, but in 1907 (see illustration), when this photograph was taken, it had just been rebuilt as two premises. At that time it was one of the more modern buildings in Kilmarnock, complete with an electric hoist and heating provided by electric radiators. John Boyle was an old-established firm in Kilmarnock, trading as drysalters since 1874. They sold various tinned and dried foodstuffs. The building had a rather ornate first floor, with various mouldings and carvings. Centrally placed, like Craig's Warehouse, which follows, was a projecting bay window, perhaps hinting at the same hand as architect. At eaves level the shop had a lively pediment, the curved walling and balustrade giving the building a sense of movement. Centrally placed over the bay window was a small pediment with carving. Boyle's shop was located next to the King Street Church, and like it succumbed to the developer in the 1960s. Today a block of modern shop premises occupies the same site.

KILMARNOCK
CHEAPSIDE STREET

Cheapside is one of Kilmarnock's oldest streets. It strikes south west from the Cross and joins Bank Street, but officially turned the corner towards the Old Bridge of Kilmarnock. This building stood on the north side of the street and was a good example of the traditional Scots domestic building, perhaps dating from the late seventeenth or early eighteenth century. Built of rubble stonework, the main façade facing the street had been rendered over, and the traditional banding created around the windows. As was common, the first-floor windows were taller than those above, indicative of this floor having more important rooms. To the rear the building had a curved frontage, containing a stair. The gables had well-eroded corbie-steps, and the slight bowing of them may indicate that the building was at one time thatched. The photograph was taken in 1973, by which time the shops on the ground floor had tried to modernise their appearance by enlarging the windows and affixing a granite frontage. The railed-off area was originally the entrance to the Crown Inn courtyard. There was quite an outcry when it was proposed to demolish this building, but the council of the time was keen to create a modern and vibrant Kilmarnock, and the building was taken down in 1980. The taller building alongside, and that at the corner also were flattened, and more modern business premises were erected on the site, built of the alien facing brick.

KILMARNOCK
CO-OPERATIVE STORE

Kilmarnock Co-operative was one of the largest co-operative societies in Scotland, and was very keen by producing buildings of architectural notice to emphasise its importance. In the centre of Kilmarnock a number of former Co-op buildings survive, now converted to other uses, such as the East Ayrshire Council offices. A number of other buildings have been lost, such as the Portland Street furniture and grocery warehouse, seen in the illustration (April

Top. Cheapside Street in Kilmarnock.
Above. Former Co-operative premises in Kilmarnock.

1988). Built of Ballochmyle sandstone, the premises were opened in November 1905. The grocery shop was located on the ground floor, the furniture department on the upper floors. The façade facing Portland Street was a rather fine example of modern Renaissance, rising four storeys in height to double gables, on which were carvings of figures representing 'Industry' and 'Justice'. It also sported some Glasgow-style wrought ironwork. The architects, Andrew and Newlands, a partnership of Gabriel Andrew (1851–1933) and William Newlands, designed most of the Kilmarnock Co-op buildings of this time and this building was by them also. Like much of Portland Street, this former store has been demolished to allow the erection of the present commercial premises, little more than utilitarian steel framed boxes, dressed thinly with a frontage of coloured concrete blocks, and lacking the skill of the mason to create a building that is both functional and an ornament to the town.

KILMARNOCK
JOHN CRAIG'S WAREHOUSE

There have been many fine major shop buildings that have been lost in the towns of Ayrshire due to town centre redevelopments. One of these was the warehouse belonging to John Craig & Son, who traded at 49–51 Portland Street

John Craig's Shop in Kilmarnock.

in Kilmarnock. The building was a grand renaissance structure, noted for its large glazed areas facing onto the street. The ground floor was originally occupied by three premises, of which Craig had two, the large areas of glass surrounded with ornate timber frames, shaped at the top. Craig also occupied the whole of the first and second floors, which again had numerous windows facing the street. The second floor windows were arched, those on the first floor being rectangular, but between these was a tall bay window, projecting slightly on the façade. The windows on this were arched, and had small leaded panes, adding the appearance of an eastern temple. Over the top of this bay was an ornate pediment containing a semicircular window and ornate finials. Before moving into this building, which they did in the early years of the twentieth century, Craig had premises further down the street, at number 43. They sold a large variety of household items, from carpets and bedding to furniture and window dressings. One of their specialities was carpet beating. Prior to demolition, this building was occupied by Times Furnishing and Henderson & Mackay insurance brokers, the ground-floor façade having long lost its attractive Victorian detailing.

KILMARNOCK
CROWN INN

Thomas Smellie drew the sketch shown here in 1922, just before these old buildings were about to be demolished. Smellie (1860–1938) was born in Partick, where his father, John Smellie, was an engineer and architect, and he grew up to become an architect in his own right. He joined Gabriel Andrew in Kilmarnock but set up on his own in 1889, and designed a number of important buildings and villas in the town. The buildings shown were part of the Crown Inn or Hotel, known also for a time as the Turf Inn. The Crown Inn was located in the Strand, which was the original old High Street of Kilmarnock, prior to the creation of new main thoroughfares in the nineteenth century. The street linked Cheapside and the Old Bridge with the north. The low buildings were of considerable age, and were perhaps erected after a disastrous fire that destroyed much of this part of the town in 1668. The external stairway led to the first floor, from which the rest of the Crown Inn (which occupied the building with the gable behind) could be reached. Where the doorway with the sign indicating 'Stabling' is located was formerly the site of a lane that led to a courtyard, but in 1886 this lane was built over with the erection of the three-storey building seen here.

Top. Sketch of the old Crown Inn in Kilmarnock.
Above. The west end of Duke Street in Kilmarnock,
with statue of James Shaw in foreground.

KILMARNOCK
DUKE STREET

The large Tudor Gothic shop premises at the corner of Kilmarnock's Duke Street and Regent Street must be one of the greatest losses any Ayrshire town centre has suffered. A magnificently sculpted and over-the-top building, it helped to give this street the epithet, 'the street of fairy castles with little turrets'. Duke Street was a Victorian improvement to the town centre. Previously travellers entering Kilmarnock from the east did so from London Road, before cutting off along Braeside Street and dropping into the town centre by way of Back Lane. A wider route was opened when Green Bridge was built, allowing London Road to reach the west side of the Kilmarnock Water, and allowing travellers to reach the cross by the wider Waterloo Street, obviously redeveloped after the battle of that name. In 1859 a number of old dwellings were demolished to facilitate the formation of a new street linking the Green Bridge with Kilmarnock Cross. Part of this followed the line of the narrow David's Lane. Originally to be known as Victoria Street, by the time it was opened it was named Duke Street, after the Duke of Portland. The street was officially opened on 25 November 1859, although on that morning there were no plans for any ceremony. However, the councillors decided that something should be done to mark the new street, so Provost Archibald Finnie, magistrates, town councillors, Commissioners of Police and trustees for the improvement of the town assembled in the town hall, from where they marched in a procession to the Cross. They then walked the length of the new street to Green Street, before turning back to the Cross. There the Provost thanked everyone for accompanying him, and he publicly named the street after the Duke, who was given three cheers. Back at the town hall the dignitaries toasted the new street with champagne. Sales of the various properties had been ongoing throughout 1859, and by the end of the year a number of buildings were almost compete. The architect of the street itself is thought to have been William Railton, of Kilmarnock, although many of the buildings within it may have been by other hands. The Tudor Gothic building shown in the illustration was perhaps his work, but it is very reminiscent of the City of Glasgow Bank by John Thomas Rochead (1814–78) in that city's Trongate. If Railton *was* the architect, then Rochead's building must have heavily influenced him – it was erected in 1854. The Duke Street building is thought to have been erected in 1861 and was demolished in 1973. James Ingram, a noted Kilmarnock architect, is known to have designed at least one building in the street. The whole of Duke Street was removed in the 1970s, to allow the erection of the fairly typical modern town-centre shopping mall. This was originally designed by Hay Steel MacFarlane & Associates and erected between 1974 and 1980, but it has been rebuilt internally since.

KILMARNOCK EXCHANGE

The Exchange Buildings in Kilmarnock stood at the junction of Portland Street with Fore Street, at Kilmarnock Cross. Three storeys in height, the lower floor of the building was finished in a dark colour. On the first floor, at the south-ernmost part of the curved frontage, was a fine Venetian window, with oversailing arch, similar in style to a number of Ayrshire country houses. The architect is unknown. The building probably dated to around 1804, when Portland Street was first built, creating a new wide street to replace the old lanes of the town. Inside, on the ground floor, was a reading room, one end of which was rounded, taking the shape of the external walls. A large rounded cantilevered stairway led up to the first floor. The Exchange Building Company ran the premises, the 1848 president being John Andrew. The Exchange was later converted into commercial premises when the new Corn Exchange was erected at the junction of Green Street and London Road in 1863. William Rankin, followed by his successor, James Bryce & Sons, wine and spirit merchants, occupied the ground floor of the old exchange. The Exchange buildings were demolished in 1937 to permit the erection of a new branch of the Royal Bank of Scotland, opened in 1939. W.K. Walker Todd designed this building, which survives, its blonde sandstone façade and copper-domed tower trying to retain the dignity of a much-altered Cross.

KILMARNOCK
HOOD STREET

Three blocks of flats, located on three sides of a square to the west side of Hood Street, of which it formed numbers 21 to 31, were erected in 1904 by the whisky company, Johnnie Walker & Sons, for its employees. Each block was three storeys in height and contained six flats. These homes were models of their time, with large areas of glazing in the public rooms, the Georgian windows being gently arched, and a variety of styles of smaller windows on the staircase. Each block had two main entrances, on a slightly projecting bay, the doors adorned with carved hoodmoulds. The bays were different in style, rising

Top. Kilmarnock Exchange at Kilmarnock Cross.
Above. Walker's Buildings in Hood Street, Kilmarnock.

above the wide-eaved roofs and finished in different parapets. The architect of the houses is not known, but it has been speculated that they were the work of Gabriel Andrew, who is known to have designed many of Johnnie Walker's Kilmarnock buildings. These include the large whisky bonds in Croft Street, erected in 1897. Andrew was a pupil of Robert Ingram, but set up for himself in 1875. The Hood Street houses were later to become the property of the local council, but they fell into disrepair. Proposals to demolish them were fought on the basis that the buildings were of architectural importance, but after a nine-year campaign they were razed to the ground in 1993. The site is now occupied by the car park of the Glencairn Retail Park.

KILMARNOCK HOUSE

Kilmarnock House was the town house of the Boyd family, whose principal seat was Dean Castle, just north of the town. The house was erected sometime in the second half of the seventeenth century and was a typical example of Scots domestic architecture, with small Georgian windows, large chimneys and crow steps on the gables. What made Kilmarnock House more refined than many other large town houses was its use of Venetian windows. There were three sets of these on the main façade, but the two on the left of the front may have been added when the house was extended sometime between 1740 and 1745. One of the Venetian windows was actually the principal doorway to the house, the other two being located on top of each other, rather over doing the ornamentation. The 4th Earl of Kilmarnock, William Boyd (1704–46), was abroad when his castle went on fire, leaving it a ruinous shell. On his return to Scotland he set up home in this house, although he was to marry the heiress of Callendar House near Falkirk, where he spent much of his time thereafter. He was an ardent Jacobite, supporting Bonnie Prince Charlie, and lost his head for the cause when he was hung, drawn and quartered in London. After his execution, the new wing to Kilmarnock House was left incomplete and shut off. At a later date a new passage was being created in the house and the workmen found the new windows for the extension, complete with wood shavings and a joiner's apron, all hidden behind a screen. Kilmarnock House originally sat in its own extensive grounds on the south-western edge of the town, but over time it became surrounded by an ever-expanding community. The grounds were gradually built on until the house was left in what was little more than a large garden, surrounded by iron railings. The house had lost its grandness, and by now was little more than a slum. In 1894 the landowner, Lord Howard de

Kilmarnock House.

Walden, gifted the house to the burgh for use as an industrial, or ragged school, the grounds becoming Howard Park. The house was eventually demolished in 1935 and the ground used as a car park for the adjoining court house, which had been erected in 1852 to plans by William Railton.

KILMARNOCK
NATIONAL BANK OF SCOTLAND

There were two major bank premises in Kilmarnock's King Street, the National Bank of Scotland at number 26 and the Commercial Bank. Both of these buildings were distinguished by their use of massive pillars at first- and second-floor levels, enclosed within the façade of the bank. The National Bank of Scotland was located at the corner of Market Lane, and was a veritable Georgian temple. It was erected sometime between 1890 and 1900. The ground floor had three arched windows forming an arcade. At first-floor level a balcony between huge side walls, built of rusticated masonry quoins, was surmounted

Top. National Bank of Scotland in Kilmarnock's King Street.
Above. The original premises of Thomas Stewart in Kilmarnock's Regent Street.

by twin pillars, rising magnificently to Corinthian capitals. There was an ornate balustrade at roof level, with corner turrets. The bank was probably too tall and narrow for its site, for there were no long views of its magnificent frontage to be had, and Market Lane was little more than a narrow passage. The bank was later to become a branch of the Royal Bank of Scotland. The Commercial Bank was located further down the street, but it lacked a corner site, being positioned midway between Back Lane and Mill Lane. This bank had a simpler frontage, the ground floor having tall windows, over which were two fluted columns, supporting an ornamented entablature. Both these banks were to be demolished in the 1970s to make way for modern shop premises.

KILMARNOCK
REGENT STREET

This old tenement building stood in what was part of Regent Street, but once Duke Street was opened up it became detached from the rest of the street. Duke Street is seen passing by the left side of the building, but originally there were more buildings there. The shop, which was occupied at the time of the photograph by Thomas Stewart & Sons' furniture and ironmongery store, was a fairly typical example of old Scots burgh architecture. The main building was three storeys in height, and the high pitched roof with corbie-stepped gables contained further rooms in the attic. A narrow close or pend passed through the lower door on the right of the ground floor to an open lane behind, where further buildings occupied the ancient back-riggs. One of the buildings in this lane was the Star Hotel, or Star Inn, which could also be reached by a pend from Waterloo Street. It was in John Wilson's printworks in Star Inn Close that Robert Burns' *Poems Chiefly in the Scots Dialect*, better known as the Kilmarnock Edition, was printed on 31 July 1786. Today all these lanes have been removed, and the site of Wilson's printworks is marked by a plaque within the doors of the Burns Mall shopping centre.

KILMARNOCK
STEWART'S FURNITURE WAREHOUSE

The old building occupied by Thomas Stewart was pulled down around 1870 to allow the erection of the fine Victorian commercial premises shown in the illustration. Writing in 1880, Archibald Mackay, in his *History of Kilmarnock*, noted that 'the recent erection, by Messrs Thomas Stewart & Sons, ironmongers, of an imposing range of buildings, comprising the new Royal Hotel, shops and warehouses, has completed [Duke] street. The architectural beauty displayed in the design of these, and the other buildings there erected, entitles it to be ranked as one of the finest streets of the town.' How things change! The street has been totally removed, so that today only a passage through the Burns Mall indicates the line of the street, with a subway linking the east end of the mall with the Palace Theatre and London Road. A bank, latterly the Clydesdale Bank, occupied the premises on the left ground floor. The Royal Hotel was located in the building to the rear of this block, but closed in 1915. The building shown was demolished in the 1970s with much of the town centre, to be replaced by faceless brick-built flat-roofed boxes, utilitarian as far as shop premises are concerned, but lacking the impressive dignity that many of the old Kilmarnock buildings once displayed.

LARGS
CURLINGHALL

The builder of Curlinghall named it in honour of his favourite sport. Dr John Cairnie was an aficionado of the roaring game, and he was instrumental in founding Largs Curling Club in 1813. He was also responsible for establishing the Royal Caledonian Curling Club in 1838, and became its first president. On 26 May 1838 Cairnie placed an advertisement in the *North British Advertiser* inviting curlers to a public meeting in the North British Hotel in Edinburgh. Around a dozen men turned up, but as no one was taking charge they began to think they had been the subject of a hoax. However, Cairnie appeared late and was able to save the meeting and have the club established. The club still acts as the world governing body for the sport. Cairnie built Curling Hall, as it was originally called, in 1812, as his home, and within its grounds he had the first artificial curling rink built in Scotland. The architect of the house was David Hamilton. After Cairnie died the house was later occupied by John Clark, Provost of Largs, who owned the Anchor Thread Mills in Paisley and who also donated the Clark Memorial Church to the town. Clark added two wings to the house between 1883 and 1889. The building was later converted to a hotel, and in 1957 the neighbouring Marine Hotel (formerly Barra House) and Curlinghall were linked to form the Marine and Curlinghall Hotel. The hotel was closed in recent years and in 1984 it was demolished. The site is now occupied by the Curlinghall flats.

Top. The later premises of Stewart's at Kilmarnock Cross.
Above. Curlinghall House, Largs.

LARGS
THE MOORINGS

Although many of Ayrshire's coastal towns were popular resorts for holiday-makers, their architecture failed to keep pace with the changing demands of the twentieth century. Most of the buildings associated with holidays dated from the late nineteenth century, such as the large hotels or recuperation homes which were erected in a variety of locations, catering for an already ageing clientele. The twentieth century, with its wars and depressions, meant that many of these institutions failed to survive, or else ambled on, their furnishings and appearance gradually becoming more shabby. When the British holiday-makers again found that they had leisure pounds in their pockets, the lure of the sun was to overtake Ayrshire as a place to relax. One of the few buildings of the twentieth century to rise to the occasion was 'The Moorings' in Largs,

The Moorings café and restaurant in Largs.

designed in an Art Deco style. Standing proudly at the foot of the Main Street, The Moorings looked onto Largs Pier, where boats sailing 'doon the watter' would call, and this was the first building to greet them. The architect was James Houston (1893–1966), who was renowned for his modern approach to buildings. He set up practice in Kilbirnie and produced drawings for buildings erected from Galloway to Glasgow. At Largs he adopted a nautical theme, The Moorings being distinguished by its arched doorways and balconies at the corner, looking not unlike the prow of an Atlantic liner. The white façades and the railings at second floor level added to this appearance, creating a building that exuded the charm of a coastal holiday and lured the tourist inside to enjoy the luncheons offered in its café and restaurant, and dances in the ballroom. Built in 1935–36, The Moorings displayed much of what was then in vogue – the steel-framed horizontal windows, glass veranda and clean repetitive lines. The Moorings were built for the Castelvecchi family on the site of an older café. During World War II it was used as HMS *Copra*, the Combined Operations Pay, Ratings and Allowances unit, employing over 600. The building was demolished in the late 1980s and a new block constructed on the same site, retaining the name 'The Moorings'. This was designed by MacMillan and Cronin of Largs and erected between 1987 and 1991 for Paul Castelvecchi. It contains 33 apartments and penthouses, with 5 commercial premises on the ground floor.

LARGS
UNDERBANK HOUSE

The original house of Underbank was erected in Greenock Road in Largs in 1873 for the Holms Kerr family, one of a number of large houses and villas built for the well-to-do along the Ayrshire coast. A very severe Gothic-style house, it was softened only by its Dutch gable. In style the house was reminiscent of the work of David Hamilton, with its Gothic-arched windows, eaves-level pediments, and entrance doorway with armorial panel over. The Holms Kerr family owned Underbank until the 1920s. In 1936 a massive addition was built out from the main entrance seen in the illustration, complete with sun-lounge, and the building was renamed the 'Hollywood Hotel'. Shortly after this the War Office requisitioned it and used it as the headquarters of Combined Operations, known as HMS *Warren*. It is claimed that 'Operation Rattle' which decided that the opening of the Second Front should take place in Normandy, was planned here, in the conference room that had been created out of the

Top. Underbank House, Largs.
Above. Mauchline House.

swimming pool, the pool being covered over. When peace resumed the Scottish Co-operative Wholesale Society acquired the building and converted it into a convalescent home. This was closed in 1982, after which the whole building was demolished and new flats erected in its place, retaining the names 'Underbank' and 'Hollywood'.

MAUCHLINE HOUSE

The old 'Place' of Mauchline, or Mauchline House as it was also known, was located in the centre of the village. Other than its Venetian window and ornate doorway, this house would not merit a second glance in most other towns, as it was a very undistinguished Georgian structure, more like a block of terraced houses than a major dwelling. However, when built, Mauchline House was one of the largest and most modern mansions in the county, and it is said that it dated from 1756, being built by the Earl of Eglinton. It had two prominent chimneys on the roof, which had a distinctive bell-cast. On the north-east side of the house, facing High Street, was an arched gateway into the Place's stable courtyard. This itself was a rather peculiar structure, with a flattened arch beneath a crenellated wallhead. To either side were distinctive ogival-capped windows. By 1858 the house was regarded as a 'disgrace to the town'. In its later twilight years, Mauchline House was divided into a number of dwellings, and even had a grocery and fish and chip shop within it. The house was eventually demolished in the 1930s. From 1965 an incongruous brick-built post office building occupied the site of the house, but this was demolished and the present library and flatted building erected in its place in 1996.

MUIRKIRK
IRONDALE HOUSE

Irondale House was erected in Muirkirk in 1790 as the 'Great New Inn' at the junction of the main roads linking Ayr with Edinburgh on an east–west axis, and Glasgow to Dumfries on a north–south axis. The latter road was only completed in 1793, and was expected to become a major cross-country route, but it never took off, and today it peters out into a footpath south of Muirkirk. The inn building was three storeys in height, and was built from coursed masonry. Three bays in width, the two outer bays had tripartite windows, over which was a flattened arch, carved from a solid lintel. The entrance doorway had stone pillars, separating the door from long narrow windows to either side. The ground and first floors were of a similar height, the second floor being lower, and the windows were much smaller. Over all was a low-pitched hipped roof. At one time it had stables located to the west of the building, where horses could be changed. Fairly Adamesque in style, the bulk of the house stood rather imposingly at the top of Furnace Road, facing the ironworks. The inn closed around 1880 and was converted into a home for the manager of the ironworks at Muirkirk, taking the name Irondale from that time. When the ironworks closed, the building became a doctor's surgery, but by 1959 it was lying empty and, with no one interested in its purchase, it was demolished in 1960. The new Muirkirk Primary School was erected to the rear of the premises in 1970.

Irondale House at Muirkirk.

Chapter 6
PUBLIC BUILDINGS

ARDROSSAN
EGLINTON SCHOOL

Built at the top end of the town's Glasgow Street, Eglinton Public School was the work of the Kilmarnock-born but Glasgow-based architect, Alexander Adamson (1842–93). Ardrossan and Saltcoats School Board had employed him to produce plans for new schools in Ardrossan parish and his Argyle School of 1876 still survives in Saltcoats (now known as Caledonia Primary School), another example of his use of the French Gothic style. The Eglinton Public School building cost £7,500 to erect and was one of the finest public schools in the county at the time. Gothic in style, the school was dominated by its central tower, which, though quite small in area, was a distinctive feature at the top end of the town with its French pavilion roof, surmounted with wrought iron work. As with most public schools of the period, the building was symmetrical around this central tower, creating boys' and girls' wings. The ends of the main

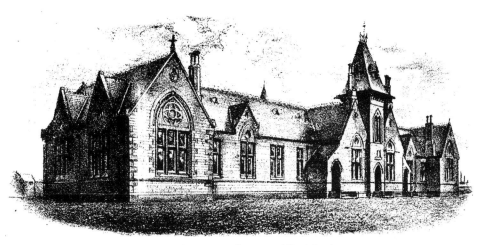

Ardrossan's Eglinton Public School.

façade had gables facing the street, over the windows of which were Gothic arches containing decorative carvings. Originally the school could accommodate 565 pupils. Eglinton School closed in 1962 but the building survived for a number of years, in 1968 taking in excess pupils from St Peter's R.C. Primary. It was subsequently demolished, the stone being used to fill in part of the harbour to create a new car park. Flatted dwellings now occupy the site.

AYR ACADEMY

What has been termed the 'old' academy in Ayr was built between 1798 and 1799 on the Burgh School Green. The old Burgh School had been established in a former cottage in 1602, and its playing green was selected as the site for the new building. John Robertson (fl. 1795–1806) of Glasgow was chosen as the architect, and he produced a classical building, then very much in vogue for modern schools. Robertson was the nephew of the famous architects, John and Robert Adam, and he is known to have completed some of their work. The Adam influence is obvious in the academy plans. The contractor was James Miller and the building was erected at a cost of £3,000. The school was opened in stages from July 1799 until January 1800. The academy was built in two storeys, the central block being taller than the rest. This contained the lofty hall, which had a gallery. There was also a small observatory, furnished with £300-worth of telescope, orrery and other equipment. The building was described as 'plain and not very ornamental', but it had more decoration than the contemporary Irvine Academy. The two wings had arched doorways, flanked with paired pillars, and the ground floor of the central block was also adorned with arched openings. On the first floor of the central block the windows had pediments and in the centre of the façade was a carved plaque. The school lasted for eighty years, by which time the fabric and fittings were dilapidated. Ayr Burgh School Board had by then been formed, and it was determined to erect a new school. Thus Messrs Clarke and Bell of Glasgow were commissioned to design the present building, erected in 1879–80 at a cost of £9,000.

AYR BARRACKS

Ayr Barracks, which were renamed Churchill Barracks in 1942 in honour of Sir Winston Churchill, were located on a sizeable area of ground on the south side of the harbour. In 1794 the former Sugar House was converted for military use

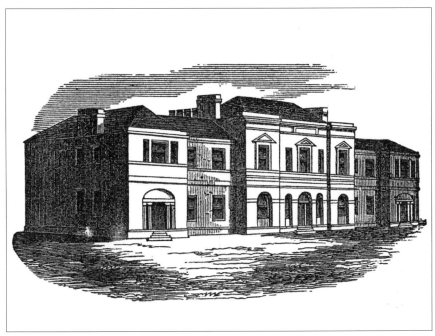

Top. The first Ayr Academy building.
Above. Ayr Barracks.

and an army camp formed, ready for action against France. When war ended in 1815 the camp was closed. In 1820, however, the barracks were rebuilt, with the 10th Hussars and 4th Royal Veteran Battalion being stationed there. A fire in the old Sugar House destroyed much of the building and a new block was erected in 1873. The barracks were then nominated as the headquarters of the Royal North British Fusiliers, Ayrshire's county regiment. This battalion was renamed the Royal Scots Fusiliers in 1881. The barracks had a number of accommodation blocks, similar in style and bulk to the one in the illustration. That one was located on a north–south axis, and the picture shows its western side. In 1959 the R.S.F. was merged with the Highland Light Infantry to form the Royal Highland Fusiliers, having the Redford Barracks near Edinburgh as its base. Ayr barracks were closed at that time, and soon the buildings were demolished. On the site Ayr Baths were erected in 1970–72, later to be joined by a number of modern blocks of flats, named in honour of former soldiers.

AYR COUNTY HOSPITAL

The old Fever Hospital, or Ayr Hospital as it had become, was seriously undersized for the demands placed on it in an ever-growing town. Plans were made for the erection of a new hospital, and a site was obtained on the south side of the River Ayr, to the east of the Kyle Union Poorhouse, erected in 1857–60 to plans by William Lambie Moffat. The new hospital was paid for by subscription, the appeal commencing in 1879, work starting in 1881, and it was proposed that the hospital should open on Christmas Day 1882. However, the completion date slipped back and it was not opened until 13 February 1883. The building cost £11,500, including furnishings and equipment. Built of

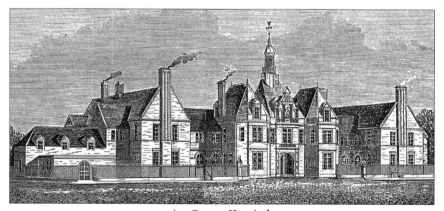

Ayr County Hospital.

Ballochmyle sandstone, the style was French Renaissance. The central block was the most ornamental, its roofs being steep and shaped to match the bays on either side of the main doorway. The highest point of the roof had a tall belfry, but this was later to be removed due to problems of maintenance. Rising up from eaves level, over the entrance, was a carving of the Good Samaritan, and over this were the arms of the burgh of Ayr. From the vestibule, doors led to a corridor which passed through the length of the building. To the right were the men's wards, leading out to a veranda overlooking the river and across to the Craigie estate. The opposite end of the hospital contained women's and children's wards. Adjoining Millbrae were the separate fever wards, which could take twenty cases. The architect of the County Hospital was John Murdoch of Ayr, a prolific worker in the town, responsible for St Leonard's Church, Alloway Public School, Smith's Institution and the Boys' Industrial School, amongst numerous commercial premises. An extension to the hospital was added to plans by James K. Hunter. Ayr County, as it was affectionately known, was closed to patients in 1991 when the modern Ayr Hospital was erected to the south-east of the town. The building remained empty for a number of years, with proposals to convert it into flats, but it was eventually demolished and new flats were erected on the site.

AYR FEVER HOSPITAL

The Fever Hospital in Ayr was built on open ground at the corner of the town's Smith and Mill streets. Suggestions for a new hospital were first mooted in 1841, following an outbreak of typhoid, and the new building was erected soon afterwards. Three storeys in height, the hospital had 20 beds initially. The main entrance was located on the first floor, flanked by pillars and reached by steps. Seven bays wide, the central three and end bays projected in front of the main block, and these three towers were higher than the rest of the building. The hospital was a good example of the Italianate villa style, with low-pitched roofs and overhanging eaves. The building stood in extensive grounds. Prior to the first patients arriving in 1844, the new building was inspected by Professor James Syme, of the department of clinical surgery at Edinburgh University. According to a report in the *Ayr Advertiser*, 'after minute inspection [he] expressed himself in very satisfactory terms in regard to the elegance of the structure, and the internal completeness and efficient management of this most useful institution.' In 1875 the hospital became a general hospital, named Ayr Hospital, and took in patients from all over the county. When the new County

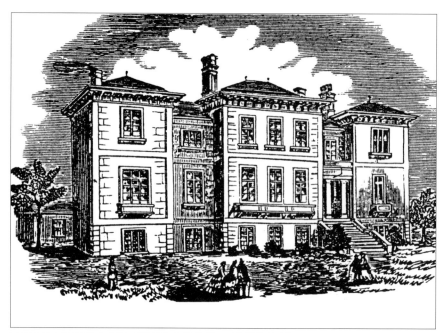

Top. Ayr Fever Hospital.
Above. The first New Bridge in Ayr.

Hospital was opened in 1883 the old hospital was closed. It was demolished soon after, and the red-sandstone tenement houses at the corner of the street were erected on part of the site.

AYR
NEW BRIDGE

Robert Burns wrote a poem entitled 'The Twa Brigs' in which Ayr's fancy New Bridge and the ancient Auld Brig argue over who is the best. The Auld Brig at one point claimed that it would still be standing when the New Bridge was 'a shapeless cairn'. This turned out to be something of a prophecy, for the New Bridge seen in the illustration (from an early photograph), turned out to be a rather weak design and it had to be taken down and replaced by the present New Bridge. The first New Bridge was designed by Robert Adam and erected between May 1786 and November 1788. A fine five-arched structure, it was adorned with four statues on the abutments, representing Bacchus, Ceres, Mars and Pan. The central two abutments had carvings of the burgh's arms. Erection of the bridge required the demolition of some buildings along the waterside, one of the earliest examples of town centre redevelopment. New Bridge Street was created as a result. The bridge cost £4,000 to build. In 1877 a severe storm resulted in the river bringing down fallen trees which battered against the structure, severely weakening it. There was little option but to take the bridge down, the Auld Brig coming back into use for a time. As Adam is one of Scotland's greatest architects and cannot be connected with a failure, it has been claimed that his design was altered by local architect Alexander Stevens, resulting in a poorer standard of build. The present New Bridge was built to engineering principles, designed by Blyth and Cunningham, and erected between 1877 and 1879 at a cost of £15,000.

AYR
OLD TOLBOOTH SITE

The older of Ayr's two tolbooths was located in the centre of the High Street, and over the years other buildings were erected against it. This created an island in the middle of what had been a wide main street, and today the buildings still create a block of architecture between the High Street and Hope Street, which is better known locally as the 'Back o' the Isle'. The old tolbooth was reputedly the place where William Wallace was held prisoner for a time, and suffered so severely that his captors thought that he was dead. They then threw his corpse out into the yard, where his nursemaid found him and took him home. Over the following months she managed to nurse him back to full health, from when he continued the struggle for Scotland's freedom. The old tolbooth was eventually demolished, and the buildings shown in a sketch of 1887 by the engraver and sculptor, Robert Bryden (1865–1939), were erected on the site. This building was built by Henry Cowan in 1810, a fairly typical example of early nineteenth-century burgh architecture, with simple Georgian windows, straight skew stones on the gable, and pillastered edgings to the shop premises below. What made the building more distinctive than the rest was the incorporation of an arched niche. In this was placed a statue of the great patriot, dressed in armour with a shield and brandishing his sword. This was sculpted by William Reid. Also incorporated in a smaller opening on the lesser gable to the left, was an ancient bust of Wallace, which had originally been part of the earlier building. Cowan's building was to be demolished in the Victorian era and a new building erected on the site. This was the work of Ayr architect Allan Stevenson, who must have been well acquainted with the site's tradition. He designed the present Scottish baronial block, all crow-steps and crenellations at roof level, with an angled turret at the corner, in 1886. Reid's original statue was incorporated in the new building, but locals claim that his legs look rather short and dumpy because the niche created for Wallace was too small to allow it to fit in and the legs had to be shortened!

The site of the old tolbooth in Ayr, with Wallace statue on façade.

AYR TOLBOOTH

Ayr's tolbooth was a tall and simple building, adorned only in its upper reaches, where it terminated in a leaded roof spire. It was located in the centre of the Sandgate, at one time the sole street of Ayr, and traffic had to pass by on either side of it. The Tolbooth dated from 1575 and contained the burgh gaol on its ground floor. An external flight of steps led to the first floor, from where a minor stair made its way through a possible further four floors to the top. Each floor was indicated externally by a string course. The accompanying reproduction of an early engraving depicts the tolbooth as an isolated tower, but there were in fact a number of lower buildings butted against it. In 1615–16 the tolbooth was altered, the public clock, ornamental spire and weather cock dating from this time. In 1754 further alterations were made to the building. The great Scots architect, Robert Adam, produced drawings for the classicising of the building in 1785, but these were not carried out. Instead, it was eventually

Early engraving of Ayr Tolbooth.

decided that the building was more of a hindrance to the town, as well as being unsafe, and it was demolished in 1826, creating the wide Sandgate we see today. At the corner of the Sandgate and High Street the new town hall and burgh chambers were erected, a massive classical building designed by Thomas Hamilton of Edinburgh. To the rear of this was the new police station and gaol. Ayr town hall is adorned with a massive spire, rising 225 feet in height.

AYR
WALLACE TOWER

The present Wallace Tower in Ayr's High Street is one of the finest urban memorials in Scotland, erected to the plans of Thomas Hamilton in 1833–34 at a cost of £2,200. It in fact occupies the site of a much older tower, one that was erected in the fifteenth century or earlier. In 1544 reference is made to the original tower as the 'Auld Tour', indicating that it was regarded as an antiquity even then. The tower was not associated with the Wallaces in its early days; indeed the earliest reference to an owner was when it was the property of Robert Cathcart of Carbieston, and it may have been his town house. A later owner was Provost Adam Ritchie who sold it to the council in 1673, who planned using it as 'ane correctione house'. The tower was rebuilt in its upper storeys in 1731, the clock and belfry being added by public subscription. In 1749 the tower was used a gaol, perhaps during reconstruction work carried out at the Tolbooth. The earliest reference to the building as the 'Wallace' Tower was in 1774, when it is thus named in a council minute. In 1808 the tower was refaced with new stone, but it was later discovered to be in an unsafe condition and was demolished in 1830. The illustration is said to depict the tower as it was in 1829.

BEITH ACADEMY

A hybrid of ecclesiastical and domestic architecture, Beith Academy was perhaps not one of the most distinguished of school buildings. And yet it had considerable charm, with its Gothic windows, strange pediment and roof ventilator. The architect was Robert Snodgrass of Beith, of whose work little seems to have survived. Perhaps his most notable buildings remaining are the Wallace Memorial at Barnweill, near to Tarbolton, erected in 1855, and the Trinity Church in Dalry, erected in 1857. Beith Academy opened on 15 March

Top. The original Wallace Tower in Ayr's High Street,
as depicted in an engraving of 1829.
Above. Beith Academy.

1875 and had accommodation for 789 pupils. It soon became too small for the children of the village and in 1930 an annexe was built in Barrmill Road. The academy was closed in 1972 with the opening of Garnock Academy in nearby Kilbirnie, at which time the building was converted into Beith Primary School. The infant department of this school remained in the building until 1 June 1999, when the pupils transferred to a new primary school built on the site of the annexe, officially opened in June 2000. The old school remained empty for a few years, suffering from vandalism, before being demolished in 2003.

BEITH
SPIER'S SCHOOL

Designed by the architect James Sellars, of Campbell Douglas and Sellars of Glasgow, Spier's School was a rather grand Scots renaissance building, dominated by its 100–foot tall clock tower. It was built in open countryside, around half a mile south east of Beith. The school was established by the Spier family, who owned the nearby Cuff and Marshalland estates, originally with the intention of being a boarding school for the poor children of Beith parish. However, by the time the school was established it had become basically a co-

Spier's School at Beith.

educational day school, but equipped to take in a few boarding students. The foundation stone was laid in September 1887 in front of more than 1,000 guests, and the Ballochmyle sandstone building was completed one year later. The first headmaster was R. Bruce-Lockhart. Sellars based the design of the school on the old Glasgow University building that stood in the High Street, but the finished seminary was not as large as that proposed by the Spier family. Nevertheless, the cost of building the school was £12,000 and it stood in 16 acres of grounds. Additions were made to the school in 1908, with the erection of a gymnasium, art and science rooms. By the 1930s the school was in financial difficulties, and in 1937 the governors passed it over to Ayrshire Education Authority. One of their first innovations was to install electric lighting. Spier's School was closed on 30 June 1972 when a modern Garnock Academy was erected at Kilbirnie, taking in secondary pupils from Spier's, Kilbirnie Central School and Dalry High School. The building stood empty for a time, with investigations being made into future possible uses. However, in the meantime the school was subject to vandalism and the whole thing was demolished in 1984.

CATRINE PUBLIC SCHOOL

The public school in Catrine was a fairly distinguished Gothic building, but one that was perhaps not the most beautiful. Built in 1860–61, the foundation stone was laid by Archibald Buchanan, who was the manager of the mill in the

Catrine Public School.

village. The school received its first intake of pupils in 1861, replacing the original Catrine Works School, which was located in an upper floor of part of the mill complex. The school building had a number of windows located in Gothic arched openings, though the windows were actually rectangular. Three main gables faced onto the street, the central one having a large rose window in it at first floor level, more suited to a church than a seminary of education. Over this rose the belfry housing the bell. The upper floor of the school was not actually completed until 1897. The school had room to accommodate 500 pupils, but in 1891 its average attendance was 391. The building to the right of the school, with its large double-storey bay window, containing proper arched windows, was the schoolmaster's house. The school was demolished early in the 1970s and all that survives of it is one of the stone pillars that formed part of the boundary wall. The remainder of the site is now occupied by private housing.

CATRINE
WILSON HALL

Almost every village had its benefactor who gifted a public hall or institute to it. Usually this was the local mill- or mine-owner who had made his fortune with the exertions of his employees; but at least many were inclined to put something back into the community, inspired to some extent, perhaps, by the

Catrine's Wilson Hall.

example of David Dale at New Lanark. In Catrine the Wilson Bequest Hall was erected in 1881–82 in the village's Bridge Street, a rather out-the-way site which had no through traffic other than pedestrians. The architect was Robert Samson Ingram. John Wilson was a baker in Catrine, and he left money in his will, dated 7 October 1872, for the erection of a hall. Unfortunately he did not leave enough money to pay for the whole building, and the community spent some time fundraising in order to have enough to build the hall, which was opened on 4 January 1882. The main hall measured 52 feet by 22 feet, able to accommodate 500 persons. The hall was used for a variety of purposes, including concerts and for cinema shows, and there was a reading room attached. The Wilson Hall was a rather French Gothic building, its tall, slated turret being its most distinctive feature. To the right of this was a pedimented façade, all built of Ballochmyle sandstone. The Wilson Hall latterly struggled to remain open, and it was taken over by the local Masonic Lodge. However, it was burnt down in the 1980s. The remains were cleared away and a sheltered housing complex occupies the site.

CUMNOCK
LADY BUTE'S HOSPITAL

Lady Gwendolyn Crichton Stuart (d. 1932), daughter of Lord Howard of Glossop and the wife of the 3rd Marquis of Bute, gifted funds to the people of

Lady Bute's cottage hospital in Cumnock.

Cumnock with which a cottage hospital was erected on Barrhill Road. Known as Lady Bute's Hospital, the building was erected in 1882 and opened in January 1883. Additions appear to have been added in 1898–99 to plans by Allan Stevenson of Ayr. Built in a traditional style, the hospital was distinguished by its numerous corbie-stepped gables. The two wings had larger windows with stone mullions and transoms. Trained nurses from the Sisters of the Sacred Heart staffed the hospital. Inside, the hospital had ten beds and three cots. Used for all sorts of medical work, the hospital was in demand to treat victims of mining accidents. Although it was established by a Roman Catholic family and staffed by nuns, the hospital was available to all. In 1920, when the Marquis stopped funding the service, the running of the hospital was passed to a committee. In 1950, after the National Health Service was established, the hospital was closed and medical services transferred to Ballochmyle Hospital near Mauchline. The building was afterwards converted into a convent, but it was demolished in the early 1970s and the site was occupied by Murray Court private housing.

CUMNOCK
PUBLIC SCHOOL

As with many public buildings in Cumnock, the Public School was the work of Robert Samson Ingram. The foundation stone was laid on 19 August 1875 and the building was erected from red Ballochmyle sandstone at a cost of £2,700. The school was opened to its first intake of pupils on 6 October 1876. The

Cumnock Public School.

school was mid-pointed Gothic in style, with depressed arches. From its elevated position on Barrhill Road, it appears as a number of tall gables, adorned with spires and finials. Some think that Ingram based the school design on that by William Lambie Moffat, who was noted for his school buildings. In Ayrshire Moffat produced the plans for the Kyle Union Poorhouse in Ayr's Holmston Road, now social work offices. On the front of Cumnock school was a small open belfry, in which was hung the bell from the old Cumnock Parish Church. This was cast in 1697 by Quirinus de Visscher of Rotterdam, but was not required, as the present parish church (erected 1863–67 to plans by James Maitland Wardrop) had new bells. For a number of years the bell hung on a tree before being housed in the school building. According to the *Ordnance Gazetteer of Scotland*, the school was 'a very elegant and commodious edifice, among the finest in the South of Scotland'. The Public School was demolished around 1974.

CUMNOCK SWIMMING POOL

Cumnock was probably one of the few towns in Scotland to have an inland outdoor swimming pool. Not so grand as the large pools at Prestwick or Troon, the pool here was originally dug by hand, the earth taken away by horse and cart. Located in the Woodroad park, just north of the town centre, the pool

Cumnock Swimming Pool.

Top. Dalrymple Public School with schoolmaster's house to right.
Above. The MacMaster Hall in Girvan.

created measured 100 feet by 45 feet, the depth of water tapering from 3 feet to 10 feet. Originally the residents of the burgh were against building a swimming pool, but eventually this was passed by a vote, the 'fors' winning 404 to 332. The cost of building the pool was £5,500 and Provost Nan Hardie Hughes opened the completed facility in June 1936. A simple building, erected as cheaply as possible, it nevertheless boasted a large terrace for spectators, in the centre of which was a fountain. Around the pool were a high wall and balcony. The pool had its water heated, something that many of the coastal outdoor pools could not match, and it was an attractive resort during the summer months when it was open. Among one of the last outdoor pools still in operation, it was closed in 2003 and demolished the following year.

DALRYMPLE PUBLIC SCHOOL

Dalrymple Parish School Board erected the public school in the village's Barbieston Road in 1875. Built of coursed rubble, the school was a T-planned single-storey building, but the double-storey schoolmaster's house was attached at one end, in bulk almost as large as the school itself. Opened in May 1876, the first headmaster was Mr J. Clark, followed by Alexander Lochhead, who was noted for writing poems. Originally the school could accommodate 212 pupils, but it was extended with the addition of further blocks to the rear in 1921. These included woodwork and cookery classrooms, taught here long before they became normal throughout the county. The school was closed in September 1962, when the present primary school was opened elsewhere in the village. The old school building survived for a time, the photograph reproduced here being taken in July 1968, but it was eventually demolished. The date stone, rescued from over the tripartite window near the photographer, was preserved in a small cairn erected on the site. Today the village community centre stands on the site of the school. The schoolmaster's house remains as a private dwelling-house and the outline of the school gable is still visible on its western wall.

GIRVAN
MACMASTER TOWN HALL

The MacMaster Town Hall was erected in 1911 to the plans of W.J. Jennings of Canterbury, the choice of architect being influenced by the fact that the person who paid for the building was John MacMaster, a banker and director in various financial institutions there. MacMaster was born at Kirkoswald but came to Girvan at the age of four. A severely classical building in the Renaissance style, the new town hall incorporated the old tower of the former town hall, which is known locally as 'Stumpy'. An earlier town hall had stood on the same site, but this was removed and the foundation stone of the new building laid in October 1909. The MacMaster Hall was erected from Giffnock freestone, the main façade adorned by a simple pediment below which was inscribed 'The MacMaster Hall'. The main entrance was reached through a simple arched portico, which led to entrance and waiting halls, from which a double stair led up to the main hall. The Lesser Hall was located beyond, on the ground floor, and could accommodate 250 people. The police court and magistrates' rooms adjoined. The main hall was located on the first floor, and complete with the gallery could accommodate 700 people. Here also was the council chamber. John MacMaster also donated £2,080 to the town council, the interest of which was to pay the caretaker. The MacMaster Hall was destroyed by fire in 1939, but with the outbreak of war little happened to the ruins. They were eventually demolished in 1956. Only the steeple of 'Old Stumpy' remains, having outlived two of its adjoining civic buildings. The tower had been erected in 1827 on the site of an older tolbooth.

GLENAFTON SANATORIUM

The outbreak of tuberculosis as a serious killer at the beginning of the twentieth century saw a public subscription raised with which to build a new sanatorium for Ayrshire. At the time over 300 people in the county were dying of the disease each year. The local health authorities joined forces to establish the hospital. A site in Glen Afton, south of New Cumnock, was chosen, for fresh air and plenty of rest were the main cure for those who suffered from the disease. Construction took almost two years, the materials being hauled up the glen from New Cumnock station by a steam traction engine. The hospital was opened in late June 1906, under the control of Dr Prest, taking in its first patients soon after. The hospital was designed by the London architect, F.G. Jones, but the Ayr architect, Allan Stevenson, was responsible on site and for some minor details. The main block was linked to the wards by enclosed corridors, and numerous balconies and large windows allowed the patients to breathe the fresh air of the glen. In the 1950s a new cure for tuberculosis, Streptomycin, was discovered, and soon sanatoriums became obsolete.

Glenafton Sanatorium.

Glenafton Sanatorium was converted into a geriatric hospital for a time, but it was closed in the 1960s. The buildings were demolished, leaving only one or two remnants, and the site was converted into a caravan and leisure park.

IRVINE ACADEMY

The old Irvine Academy was one of David Hamilton's many works in Ayrshire. Hamilton (1768–1843) is regarded as one of Glasgow's finest architects, responsible for many notable works. He produced many public buildings, churches, hospitals, theatres, banks and country houses or suburban houses in the city, but he also produced many plans for Ayrshire clients. Among those that survive are Robertland House, near Stewarton, the New Church in Ayr, Tournament Bridge at Eglinton and Kilwinning Abbey Tower. Hamilton's design for a new academy for Irvine was rather plain compared with his other work, perhaps as a result of fewer funds than originally hoped for. The foundation stone was laid on 22 April 1814 and the school was opened for its first intake of pupils on 3 July 1816. It became Irvine Royal Academy on receiving a charter from the Regent, afterwards George IV, in 1818. Two storeys in height, the building was nine bays long, the central three projecting beyond the main façade and topped with a plain and low pediment. The first floor had a string course at sill level, and the doors and windows had a simple mould around them. Otherwise the building lacked ornament. Initially the school had only three teachers, but the roll had risen to 400 by 1820. The school was demolished in 1901 to provide for the construction of a replacement building, designed by John Armour, and erected of red sandstone. This acted as Irvine Royal Academy until 1992, when it was closed, and the school merged with the 1950s Ravenspark Academy, built in Kilwinning Road. The Armour building is now occupied by offices, renamed Sovereign House.

IRVINE BRIDGE

The oldest known bridge across the River Irvine was probably erected in 1533. No doubt it was a multiple-arched structure, built of stone, rather similar to those surviving at Ayr and Dumfries. The bridge was rebuilt between 1748 and 1752, at which time the carriageway was widened to 11 feet. The council applied to the government in 1826 for 'an Act for widening and improving the Bridge of Irvine, making streets communicating thereto, and for more effectual enlarging, deepening, improving and maintaining the Harbour of Irvine'. This was granted, and rebuilding of the bridge took place in 1827, when new stone arches were erected to support a carriageway 25 ft 8 in. in width. The tolls, which were established to finance the bridge, were removed in 1850. In 1898 it was widened once more, this time in iron, to produce a carriageway of 38 ft 4 in. At the 1898 widening, the work was completed by Messrs Alexander Findlay and Company of Motherwell. The engineers responsible for the design were Messrs J. & A. Leslie and Reid of Edinburgh. At the time of erection the provost of Irvine was Andrew Watt, the Dean of Guild James Armour, and the Town Clerk James Dickie. The bridge was closed on 10 June 1973 and demolished soon after. From 1973–75 the Rivergate shopping centre was constructed, designed and built by Irvine Development Corporation, creating a covered pedestrian route across the river, vehicles being rerouted to other bridges.

IRVINE TOLBOOTH

The tolbooth in Irvine was a rather fine example of burgh architecture. A distinguished Georgian structure, adorned with arched windows and projecting quoins, the tolbooth had a tall steeple at one end, on which was a public clock and two bells. This building had been rebuilt a number of times from 1386, when a charter of King Robert II confirmed Irvine's right to erect a tolbooth. Originally this was 40 ft by 30 ft in plan, with walls 4 ft thick. The

Top. Irvine Academy.
Above. Irvine Bridge.

Top. Irvine Tolbooth.
Above. Kilbirnie Central School.

lower floor was vaulted, for strength, and the upper floor held a council chamber, reached by an internal stairway. The old bell of the tolbooth was inscribed, 'The Tolbooth Bell of the Burgh of Irvine, 1637', and a later bell had the motto, 'Blessed are they that hear the joyful sound', perhaps not applicable to the internees. A man was at one time paid to ring the bell when the town gates or ports were opened, and at nightfall when the curfew came into force. Part of the original building was probably incorporated in a rebuilding of 1745, at a cost of £745, following the original tolbooth being struck by lightning. This knocked down part of the roof, broke the public clock and caused cracks to appear in the steeple. At the same time the prison door was broken and several men may have been killed, or at least seriously injured. At one time the public gallows was located outside the tolbooth, and a woman was hanged here around 1755 for murdering her own child. Her bones were later kept in a box and used in anatomy lessons at Irvine Royal Academy. Seen in the sketch is the former tron, or public weigh machine. The tolbooth was demolished in 1860–61 when the present Town House was erected, allowing the street to be widened. The original weather vane and some carved stones were incorporated in the new building.

KILBIRNIE CENTRAL SCHOOL

One of the grandest village schools to be found in Ayrshire could be seen in the northern community of Kilbirnie. Erected in 1913–14, the Central School was built on a site at Newhouse to cope with increasing numbers of pupils in the town. The cost of the building was £8,000, but the outbreak of war held up the completion of the building, and it was not finished fully until 1921. Here maths, English, geography, history, sciences, art, practical subjects and drill were taught, along with other subjects. Distinguished by its twin towers, topped with domes and weather vanes, the school presented a fresh array of windows to the street. The central portion had a strange pediment, and in the middle of the roof was a turreted bell tower. As with most schools of its period, the building was divided into two halves, with one entrance for boys and another for girls. The school was closed in 1972, when Garnock Academy in the town was erected. The Central then became a primary school, catering for primaries one to three, but it closed in 1992 when the new Glengarnock Primary School was opened, replacing the Central School as well as the old Glengarnock School, which had been erected in 1883. Both schools were demolished in late 1992. A new health centre was erected on the site and was opened in April 1994.

KILMARNOCK ACADEMY

Following the Education (Scotland) Act of 1872 school boards became responsible for providing education for all children in their parishes. It was soon apparent that in many cases the existing schools were not of a suitable standard, and all over the country programmes of new building commenced. Some of the schools erected were of a particularly high standard architecturally, often as a result of a burgh's pride in itself. The Kilmarnock Academy erected in 1875–76 was one of those buildings which was rather over-the-top to some extent, its Gothic architecture more reminiscent of a town hall than a place of education. It was a Kilmarnock man, William Railton, who provided the plans for the school. He had an interest in historical architecture, having supplied plans of castles to David MacGibbon and Thomas Ross for their five-volume masterpiece, *The Castellated and Domestic Architecture of Scotland*. He should not be confused with the eminent London architect of the same name, responsible for Nelson's Column amongst other major works. The foundation stone of Railton's academy was laid on 20 November 1875 and in August 1876 the building was ready for its first intake. In style the Academy was a cross between Elizabethan Gothic and Tudor architecture, the main façade of the entrance block being a rich fantasy of Gothic arched windows, traceried gables, ogival-roofed turrets and a public clock. To either side were single-storey wings, less decorative in style, but echoing the elements of the main building. The cost of the school was £4,500. The building had to be extended in 1887, but within ten years it had become too small again for an ever-expanding town, so in 1898 the present Academy building was erected elsewhere in the town, to plans by Robert Ingram. The old academy became Hamilton Street Primary School, extended again in 1942; but this was closed and the building demolished.

KILMARNOCK BATHS

The public baths in Kilmarnock were erected in Titchfield Street in 1938–40 to cater for a demand for swimming in the town. The first proposals for a municipal pool had been raised in November 1930, but it was felt that the economics of the time could not allow one to be built. However, by May 1937 things had improved, and the proposal was passed. The pool was unique in Britain at the time, for it was the only one that had a wave-making machine. At each swimming session this was switched on for a time, creating nine-feet high

Top. Kilmarnock Academy.
Above. Kilmarnock Baths.

waves that made their way across the pool, splashing off the steps at the far end. The machine was designed and manufactured by the local hydraulic engineering company, Glenfield & Kennedy, and was 'presented by them to the corporation for the benefit of the people of Kilmarnock'. The company had developed the machine for the testing of model ship hulls. It was not until twenty years later that a second British pool was to have a similar set up. The pool itself was 100 feet long by 42 feet wide, contained 215,000 gallons and was officially opened on 5 October 1940. The cost of erection was £37,322 and Provost Wilson's wife performed the opening ceremony. The bathing-pool building was a rather plain structure, built of bricks, and lacking the imaginative designs so prevalent in 1930s municipal architecture. Alexander Dunlop, a Kilmarnock architect, who trained with James Miller in Glasgow, designed it. The pool was used for training commandos during the Second World War. Kilmarnock Baths were closed following the erection of the Galleon sports centre across the road, designed by Crichton Lang & Willis, and erected in 1986.

KILMARNOCK
BURNS MONUMENT

The Burns Monument in Kilmarnock actually became yet another example of Ayrshire's lost architecture just as the author was putting the final touches to this book. The building was a magnificent Gothic structure, rising 80 feet above the level of the town's Kay Park, and was visible from miles around. The building was designed by Robert Ingram, and was officially opened on 9 August 1879. It was built at a cost of £2,893. Constructed of Ballochmyle sandstone by Andrew Calderwood, the lower two floors of the memorial contained a museum of Burns artefacts. Within, a stairway made its way up through the memorial tower to a viewing platform. On the south side of the monument, protected by an arched porch, was a Sicilian marble statue of the poet by William Grant Stevenson. The complete memorial was decorated with columns, corbels, arms, balustrades and dummy shot holes. In recent years the memorial was closed due to a lack of funds, and the museum artefacts removed to the Dean Castle in 1959. Susceptible to vandalism, the council bricked up the lower windows and fenced the whole structure off in 1987, following a severe case of vandalism, supposedly to protect the listed building until funds for restoration could be found. Restoration work costing £380,000 was undertaken in the early 1990s, but for twelve years the building stood empty until early on

The Burns Monument in Kilmarnock's Kay Park.

Top. Kilmarnock Fire Station.
Above. Kilmarnock Infirmary.

Saturday morning, 20 November 2004, it was burned to the ground. Firefighters dowsed the flames, but as they did so part of the roof collapsed. The burnt out shell was left in an unstable condition, the high tower leaning precariously. Over the following couple of days much of the memorial was demolished, though fortunately the statue was undamaged and was saved.

KILMARNOCK FIRE BRIGADE STATION

The first fire brigade in Kilmarnock was in operation as early as 1753, when the town council organised a voluntary brigade to attend fires. In that year the council spent £40 to buy a specially made water cart with pump which could jet water into the air. The horse-drawn cart came with a 40-ft length of hose, but it used only water that it carried on board, so its dowsing properties were limited. In 1863 the first official 'fire brigade station' was built in Green Street, a simple brick built garage with stone dressings around the main arched doorway and side door. The name of the building was carved in stone and incorporated in the façade of the gable. Within the station there was room to store one horse-drawn water tender and some stores. In 1876 there were ten men in the fire brigade, working part time and receiving five shillings for each fire that they turned out for. A second and third station were erected in the town, at Riccarton Toll in 1884 and Calcutta Lodge in 1896. The three fire stations closed on 22 November 1937, when a new fire station was erected in Titchfield Street, designed by Gabriel Steel. This seems to have echoed the old station in style, but on a grander scale, with the use of brickwork and stone dressings, while its size allowed the incorporation of carved panels depicting the burgh arms and a fireman's helmet. Over the garage where the fire engines were stored were flats where the firemen lived and were on call 24 hours per day. This building has in turn been replaced by a third fire station at Riccarton.

KILMARNOCK INFIRMARY

The architect behind the original block of the Kilmarnock Infirmary, which was built on an elevated site at the top of Portland Street, was William Railton (1820–1902). Born in Glasgow's Gorbals, nothing is known of his early training, but it is known that he had set up his practice in Kilmarnock, his wife's home-town, by 1851. However, it has been speculated that Railton may have had some training, or else was heavily influenced by, Glasgow's second most famous architect, Alexander 'Greek' Thomson (1817–75). The Infirmary displayed a number of Greek style undertones, which were not unlike Thomson's, such as the pillared windows and the carved details on certain lintels, including antefixae and key mouldings. The foundation stone of the new hospital was laid in September 1867, and by October 1868 the hospital was ready for its first patients. The infirmary had 24 beds, and was erected at a cost of £4,146. The original building was constructed in what were the grounds of Mount Pleasant House, this erection being retained for some years as a home for administrative staff. However, in later years it was demolished and replaced by huge wings, which more than tripled the size of the original hospital. In total, additions were made to the infirmary in 1881, 1891 (Children's Block), 1893 and 1899 (Fevers Block). Always constrained by its cramped site, Kilmarnock Infirmary was closed in September 1982, when the new general hospital on a greenfield site west of the town, at Crosshouse, was opened. The building survived empty for a time, but in August 1989 it was estimated that it would cost £250,000 to repair structural faults and permission was granted for demolition. An outcry resulted in the Secretary of State overturning this decision in January 1990. There followed plans to convert it into a nursing home, but these came to nought, and the building was destroyed by fire in the summer of 1994, after which it was demolished.

KILMARNOCK
STURROCK STREET POLICE STATION

Opened on Thursday 22 September 1898, Kilmarnock Police station was one of the town's most unusual buildings. Located in Sturrock Street, which was not one of the town's principal thoroughfares, the police station succumbed to town centre redevelopment. No doubt, had the station been located in one of the other main streets in the town, it may have survived, though Kilmarnock's record in preserving interesting buildings is a poor one. The police station was an unusual example of free renaissance architecture. The front facing Sturrock Street, 60 feet in length, was perhaps over-adorned with pillars and turrets, the colonnade having seven pairs of pillars, over two levels. On the ground floor were two main doorways, with broken pediments containing elaborate carvings. Centrally placed on this front was a Flemish gable, surmounted by a statue of a lion. Behind this was a steep French-style tower, topped with an elaborate wrought ironwork crown. The hipped roof had a flat top, surrounded by railings, allowing the constables to look over the town. The other façades

Sturrock Street Police Station in Kilmarnock.

were far simpler in style, only the bands of string-courses adding to an otherwise plain front. In plan the station was irregular, taking the shape of the roadways and river surrounding its island site. Inside were eight cells on two floors and a court hall 30 feet by 20 feet. Access to the charge room was from a rear entrance in Back Lane. The building was designed by Kilmarnock architect, Walter W. Reid, of whom little is known. The station was replaced as the burgh police headquarters in 1954, but the offices continued in use until 1972 and were demolished the following year.

KILMARNOCK TOWN HALL

The residents of Kilmarnock were always a bit apologetic of their Town Hall, which stood in King Street, straddling the Kilmarnock Water. King Street was one of the burgh's major improvements made at the beginning of the nineteenth century. Previously the main north–south route in the town went by way of Sandbed Street (still a lane behind the shops on the west side of King Street, next to the water) to the top of Titchfield Street, at the junction of Fowlds and St Andrew streets. An Act of Parliament was received which allowed the burgh

Top. Kilmarnock's Town Hall.
Above. The Viking Cinema in Largs.

to arrange for the creation of a wider street to be laid out, cutting through the back courts and gardens of Sandbed Street. At the north end of this street the New Bridge was erected over the water in 1804, and later in the year King Street was opened. In 1805, on the east side of the New Bridge pillars and arches were erected over the water to create a platform on which a new Town Hall was erected. When it was opened the new building was regaled as a major improvement, but within 40 years or so, it was regarded as too small for the town. Classical in style, the Town Hall, or Town House as it was also known, suffered from the inclusion of shop premises on the ground floor, which meant that the passer-by failed to be impressed by any form of civic dignity. It was only from a distance that the pediment and arched window were noticed, and towering over the building the spire, containing the bell removed from the original burgh tolbooth. This bore the inscription: *This Bell was gifted by the Earl of Kilmarnock to the town of Kilmarnock for their Council-house. A.M. Edin. 1711.* On the ground floor, between the shops, a heavily moulded door gave access to the building. Nine bays in width, the first floor had an Adamesque recessed arch, the window of which originally led to a balcony where the dignitaries could make proclamations. However this was removed in the late nineteenth century to improve the line of the street. The central three bays projected slightly, and were topped with a pediment bearing the burgh's coat of arms. Inside the Town House, the burgh gaol was located in the basement, but in 1852 there was a major flood in the river below which would have drowned the prisoners had they not been rescued. The Town Hall was demolished in 1970 as part of the redevelopment of the town centre.

LARGS
VIKING CINEMA

James Houston of Kilbirnie was one of the most notable architects in the northern part of Ayrshire, renowned for his modern approach to architecture and his love of telecommunications. He was responsible for a few cinemas, one of which, the Radio City in Kilbirnie (opened in 1938), still stands, the subject of a major restoration in 2003 by the Radio City Association. The Viking picture-house in Largs was not so lucky, for it was demolished in 1983 and the site was developed as retirement flats, known as Homemount. The cinema was located in Irvine Road, Largs, at the junction with Gogoside Road. Originally there was a Victorian Gothic villa located here, known as Millburn House, but this was acquired and flattened to make way for the erection of the picture house. The style of the building was very distinctive, with a number of 1930s Art Deco features, but it was rather idiosyncratic, with its arched windows and heavy buttresses, supporting crenellated walls. From the main entrance, which was located up a flight of stairs, projected half a Viking longship, its prow adorned by a tall figurehead of a horse. The cinema closed on 4 August 1973 with the advent of television in almost every home, and the building was converted into a bonded warehouse for a time.

LOUDOUNHILL VIADUCT

Ayrshire has numerous railway viaducts, many of which are of historical or engineering significance. The Ballochmyle Viaduct near Mauchline has the world's longest masonry arch, a massive 180 feet in length, spanning the gorge of the River Ayr. At Cumnock the Bank Viaduct has one of the highest masonry arches in the country, 175 feet above the level of the Lugar Water below. Both viaducts are still in use by the Glasgow to Dumfries railway. Another well-known viaduct was the Loudounhill Viaduct, which crossed the valley of the infant River Irvine, to the east of Darvel. Built as part of the Strathaven and Darvel Railway branch of the Caledonian Railway Company, the viaduct was opened to passenger trains on 1 May 1905. The viaduct comprised 13 semicircular arches, built of engineering bricks, and carried the railway line from one side of the valley to the other. The line took goods traffic from 4 July 1905. The railway from Darvel to Strathaven was closed on 9 September 1939, after which the rails were lifted. The viaduct remained as a local landmark for many years, but its condition gradually deteriorated and it was decided that it should be demolished. Locals campaigned to save the viaduct, but it was blown up in 1986, not without considerable difficulty, which made a mockery of their 'unsafe' claim.

LUGAR
WEIR INSTITUTE

The village of Lugar was originally established with the erection of the ironworks in 1845. A senior partner in the company that owned the ironworks, William Weir of Kildonan, paid for the erection of the Weir Institute in the village in 1892. The architect was Robert Ingram, who produced plans for many of the buildings required by the Baird company, and he designed what was a

Top. Loudounhill Viaduct, with the volcanic plug of Loudoun Hill behind.
Above. The Weir Institute in Lugar.

rather unique building for its time. Built of white freestone, the institute had a large hall that could accommodate 350. Adjoining rooms contained a library of 582 books, located on oak shelves, each volume bound in leather, and the national newspapers and a selection of magazines were subscribed to. There was a billiards room with two tables, and a games room, where various board games were offered. There was also a skittle alley, and two summer-ice boards. And yet the most advanced facility that the institute had was a heated indoor swimming pool! This measured 50 feet in length, by 24 feet wide, and was up to 6 feet deep in places. The pool was lined with white glazed bricks, and heated by water released from the ironworks. There were diving boards and other water appliances, and swimming instruction was offered. A separate private bath was also available, the user paying an additional fee for this. Residents of Lugar were able to use the facilities of the institute for an annual subscription of half-a-crown. After the Second World War the fortunes of the institute dwindled, and the pool was covered over and converted into a dance floor. In nearby Logan, where many of the occupants of the miners' rows were rehoused, an IFE wing was erected, resulting in the institute closing in 1965. From 1966 it was used as a clothing factory for a time, but eventually this and other uses ended. The building suffered fires and partial demolition, leaving only a fragment of the institute, now incorporated into a new house.

MAYBOLE
LADYLAND SCHOOL

Prior to 1875 Maybole had five schools in the town: the parish school, three schools associated with different churches, and the industrial school. However, in 1875 work commenced on a new public school in Carrick Street which was erected at the expense of the Maybole School Board. This new school building was far more advanced and had better accommodation than the other schools, all of which closed when it opened in August 1876. The school building was a fine classical structure, more like a country house than the more usual style of board schools. It was built over two floors, and it was noted for its many arched windows. The principal front was more ornate than the other façades, with projecting bands of masonry and hoodmoulds with pronounced keystones over the lower floor windows. The windows on the upper floor were linked in pairs or threes, and had flattened arches, whereas the rest of the building had full round arches. The principal entrance was located centrally on this front, protected by a sizeable portico, complete with paired Doric columns

Ladyland School in Maybole.

supporting a balustraded balcony. The lesser fronts of the school were
unadorned with such finery, and displayed simply a regular array of arched
windows. Only the boys' and girls' entrances on the two sides had any pretence
of grandeur, with simple Georgian pavilion-like porches. Ladyland School was
the work of the Ayr architect John Murdoch. When the school opened a grand
procession of pupils made their way through the town, and at night a special
concert and dedication took place for the parents. The school had accommodation for 850 pupils, but within 25 years it was to become too small for
Maybole, and a second school had to be built in the town. This was the Cairn
School, erected in 1898 to plans by James Kennedy Hunter, with accommodation for 450. Hunter also designed some additions to Ladyland School
around the same time. Ladyland School, which was to be renamed Carrick
Academy, went on fire on Sunday 1 March 1919. Fire tenders from Maybole and
Ayr were unable to stop the blaze, which destroyed all of the building. The shell
was subsequently demolished and a new Carrick Academy was erected in
1925–27 to plans by J. St Clair Williamson.

MAYBOLE TOLBOOTH

Part of the old tolbooth of Maybole still stands, for it was incorporated in the
Town Hall building of 1887, the work of Robert Ingram. The tolbooth was
originally the town house of the Kennedy lairds of Blairquhan Castle, which

Top. Maybole Tolbooth when it was surrounded by other buildings.
Above. The Baird Institute in Muirkirk.

stands six miles to the south east. Maybole at one time had a number of town houses belonging to local lairds, the principal one remaining today being Maybole Castle, which dates from the early seventeenth century and which is still the property of the Marquis of Ailsa, chief of the Kennedy family. Blairquhan's town house dated from the early sixteenth century, but it was sold in 1674 to the Earl of Cassillis and the bailies of the burgh to be used as a tolbooth. The original building had a prominent tower, rising through various storeys to an upper couple of floors, which were added later, and which contained a public clock. Above this was a Gothic window and crenellated parapet, over which was a pyramidal roof. To one side of the tolbooth was a major wing, and on the ground floor of both this wing and the tower were doors with distinctive double arched mouldings around them. On the ground floor was the burgh gaol, and over it were the council offices. The tolbooth in Maybole was gradually shorn of its surrounding buildings – those on the right in the illustration (from an old sketch), to facilitate road widening, and the main block to the left to accommodate the erection of the present town hall. The original clock was removed and a new one incorporated in a French-style roof that replaced the original.

MUIRKIRK
BAIRD INSTITUTE

The Baird Institute in Muirkirk was erected in 1887 as a gift from local landowner and director of the ironworks, Colonel John G.A. Baird, MP, who lived at the now lost Wellwood House. The cost of the building was in excess of £2,000, but it was a great boon to the remote village. Within it were a reading room, recreation room, library, committee room, caretaker's room and other facilities. Many local societies met in the institute, and it was a popular rendezvous for playing billiards, snooker, carpet bowls and other games. Attendance, however, began to wane, and the committee threatened to close the institute, but from 1950 onwards it began to rise and the institute was reprieved. In 1954 a special meeting of the trustees decided that due to rising costs the institute should be closed, and the title returned to the superior at the end of the year. Negotiations commenced with the Scottish Youth Hostels Association, who had expressed an interest in taking it over as a hostel, but eventually they decided not to proceed. The building was demolished in October 1957 and the site of it, at the gates to Victory Park, is now public open space.

PRESTWICK SWIMMING POOL

The swimming pool at Prestwick was built at the northern end of the town's esplanade. Erected at a cost of £37,000, the pool was the largest in Scotland when it was opened in June 1931 by William Adamson, Secretary of State for Scotland. The architect was William Cowie. The bathing pond was a hundred yards in length, making it Olympic standard, and it could accommodate a million gallons of water. The shore side was curved, the widest part of the pool being forty-three yards broad. Unfortunately this was unheated, which was to result in the pool's demise. It had two chutes and two diving boards. The buildings were rather grand, two large pavilions at either end being roofed with domes. Along one side of the pool was a long colonnade, sheltering the spectators. The pool could accommodate 1,200 bathers and a further 3,000 spectators, and in its first year 321,855 people paid it a visit. However, with dwindling attendances the cost of running the facility was prohibitive. One of its last highlights was staging the BBC's 'It's a Knockout' in May 1971. The pool was closed in 1972 and most of the structure was pulled down in 1982. At one time there were plans to create a large aquarium and seal sanctuary in the building, but this never came to fruition. Part of the sea wall and the empty pool survive, now used as a play area.

SALTCOATS BATHING STATION

The bathing station at Saltcoats was one of the earliest organised public swimming areas in the county. On the headland to the west of Saltcoats harbour, opposite the grand villas of Winton Circus, was a natural pool that was left isolated when the tide receded. This pool was surrounded by flat bedrock, and for many years was a popular spot for swimming. On the headland on the southern side of the pool a bathing house was erected in 1894, to allow bathers to change their clothes, and for other facilities. The station was built rather like traditional Scots cottages and, apart from the balcony on the far end of the buildings, reached by an external stairway, did not promote itself as a leisure centre. In 1933 the ponds at Saltcoats were redeveloped, with new concrete walls to hold three permanent pools, the waters of which were refreshed from the sea. This was to be the largest tidal pool in Scotland at the time, and was popular with locals and holidaymakers alike, to whom Saltcoats was a coastal resort. In the 1940s considerable extensions were added, enclosing the pool further with flat-topped buildings on top of which were

Top. Prestwick Swimming Pool.
Above. Saltcoats Bathing Station as first built.

Top. Skelmorlie Hydropathic Hotel.
Above. Stevenston Public School.

balconies. The popularity of the pool declined and it was eventually closed. A shellfish grower used the pools for a time, but this business closed and the pools were demolished in 1985.

SKELMORLIE HYDRO

At one time one of the grandest hotels on the north Ayrshire coast, Skelmorlie Hydropathic Hotel was erected in 1868–73 in the Scottish baronial style, which was then in vogue. Mainly four storeys in height, the hotel was adorned with turrets and tower, string courses and corbie-stepped gables. Built of a rough-dressed coursed sandstone, it rose from the top of the cliff that separates Upper and Lower Skelmorlie. At one corner a four-square tower with adjoining cylindrical stair-tower rose through five storeys to a high viewing platform, surrounded by an open balustrade. Dr Ronald Currie, who was a member of Professor Joseph Lister's surgical class in Glasgow, established the hydro. When opened it offered Turkish, salt-water and other bathing pools. In 1931 the hotel changed hands for £3,500, the new syndicate of Glasgow businessmen enlarging the dining room and erecting the 'vita-glass' roofed palm court. To aid guests arriving at the lower half of the village a mechanical lift was built up the cliff-side in 1941. One of the syndicate, Robert Davidson, would be in charge at the hotel. During the war the hotel was used for billeting Wrens, and further accommodation was found in Nissen huts located in the grounds. The former Prime Minister, Earl Attlee, was a guest at the hotel in 1950 and 1951. Skelmorlie Hydro suffered a fire in 1977 and was closed in 1984. After lying empty for a time it was demolished in 1987.

STEVENSTON PUBLIC SCHOOL

The public school in Stevenston adopted a fairly standard layout for schools of the period, whereby the central block contained the main entrance, adorned with a tower or other enriched architectural detailing. To either side of this were wings, often terminating in lesser towers, or in the case of Stevenston, in blocks built at right angles to the main length of the school, the gable facing the street giving the height. The school was located in New Street, which heads south from the town centre towards Ardeer. Shortly after the passing of the Education Act in 1872, proposals were quickly made for a new school in the town. A local architect, Hugh Thomson, provided the plans. The building was completed and the first pupils made their way into the classrooms in 1875. The school's central tower was one of its main features, complete with a steeply pitched French-style roof, topped with elaborate wrought ironwork. Over the windows on the principal gables were rope mouldings, the other windows being simple openings with mullions and transoms, complete with lying panes. The school served as a Higher Grade school until August 1971, when the new Auchenharvie Academy was opened, after which it served as Stevenston Primary School. In 1982 the school was gutted by fire, and it was demolished. On the site a new primary school, named Glencairn Primary, was built, incorporating the date stone from the old school.

TROON SWIMMING POOL

The swimming pool at Troon was located in Titchfield Road and opened to the public in 1931. A simple classical building, the pool complex was rather Roman in style externally, with large arched pavilions at the external corners. Some of the decorative parts were of an Art Deco style. During the Second World War the Commandos used the pool for training. There were a number of attempts made at trying to heat the water, but the lack of a roof meant that this was virtually impossible. A new indoor swimming pool was built in Troon in 1987 and the old pool closed. The pond was filled in with the demolished buildings, and the whole site now forms a car park.

Troon Swimming Pool.

CHAPTER 7
INDUSTRIAL BUILDINGS

AUCHINLECK
BARONY COLLIERY

William Baird & Company sank two shafts on Oldbyres farm, to the west of Auchinleck, and created the Barony Colliery in 1906. The pit was complete and producing its first coal in 1912, doing this by methods modern at the time. The longwall advancing technique was used, and the coal was brought to the surface in large tubs on an endless rope, each capable of holding 11 cwt. At the time the pit employed 871 men below ground, with a further 203 on the surface. In 1938 the pit was reorganised, with the intention of increasing output. A third shaft was sunk at this time, and new electrical winding gear installed. The outbreak of war held up progress for a number of years, but by 1946 the third

The Barony Colliery at Auchinleck, with the winding frame that survives.

shaft reached a depth of 2,052 feet below the surface. On 8 November 1962 Number 2 shaft collapsed, and the winding frame partially fell into the hole. Four men were trapped below ground, but there was no way of getting them out. Their bodies remain interred there to this day, and they are among those commemorated on a memorial stone erected nearby. The bulk of the pit's 1,614 workers had to be laid off, and shafts numbered one and two were filled in. A new shaft was created, but it was four years in the making at a cost of £2,000,000. The pit continued to work until 1989, when it was eventually closed. Some of the older pithead buildings had been listed by Historic Scotland, but by this time it was too late, and the buildings were all demolished. All that remains today is the massive winding frame, kept as a monument to those who were killed in the struggle for coal.

AUCHINLECK
BARONY GENERATING STATION

The power station located adjacent to the Barony Colliery in Auchinleck parish was quite unique in its design. It was the first power station in the country that was able to burn a low quality coal slurry and convert it into electricity, or 'a modern alchemist's dream come true', according to John Maclay, the Secretary of State for Scotland, who opened the works on 11 October 1957. Previously coal washings and dross were of little use, and ended up piled in coal bings that disfigured much of the Ayrshire coalfield. The power station had been developed to take this waste and use it to generate electricity. Once the slurry had been burned all that remained was a fine dust, of less bulk, which could then be dumped. This dust, however, earned the station the local nickname, the 'Stoor Factory'. Work on the station started in 1955, soon after the nationalisation of the electricity generating industry, and after two years the first electricity was produced. Unfortunately, plans to use the large bing at Barony Colliery proved to be fruitless, due to it not being suitable, so coal waste had to be obtained from other sites. The contractors for the power station were Babcock and Wilcox Ltd and the client was the South of Scotland Electricity Board. Two cooling towers 200 feet high were constructed, and a chimney of 265 feet was added. Water for cooling was taken from the Lugar Water at Ochiltree, where the dam was rebuilt. Inside were two 30,000 kW generators, which required 150,000 tons of slurry per annum. The cost of construction, at £10,500,000, was more than twice the estimate. When coal slurry became more difficult to get, with the closure of pits and increasing costs of transport, the

The Barony Generating Station at Auchinleck.

power station was closed in 1982. The two cooling towers were blown up in 1983, the tall chimney in 1986, and the site cleared thereafter.

AUCHINLECK
HIGHHOUSE COLLIERY

The Highhouse Colliery was sunk on the edge of the village of Auchinleck in 1894 to mine coal. Grant, Ritchie & Co. Ltd of Kilmarnock made the winding engine in 1896, and it hauled up its first coal the same year. Known as 'Auld Ben', the engine made a distinctive sound that could be heard throughout the village. It produced 65 horsepower, and was capable of raising coal from the pit bottom to the surface in 15 minutes. Some of this coal came from a seam that had so few impurities that it burned to produced little ash. It was known as 'Highhouse Jewel' coal. On 22 July 1908 a serious fire erupted in the pit, affecting production. This was brought under control, and after some rebuilding production resumed. In 1910 there were 514 miners working in the seams, with a further 80 on the surface. This number gradually decreased over the years, as the seams became worked out. Some improvements at the pit were made in 1959, when a new winding engine was installed. 'Auld Ben' was

Top. Highhouse Colliery at Auchinleck.
Above. A view of Mill Street tanneries in Ayr.

then dismantled and taken to the Heriot-Watt College in Edinburgh for preservation. In 1983 the mine was closed, and work commenced on stripping the buildings. Only the headframe survives, and one or two smaller buildings, converted into small industrial units.

AYR
MILL STREET TANNERIES

The tanneries in Mill Street, Ayr, were owned by two different companies. The building in the centre of the illustration, with the arched windows and doors on the ground floor, was owned by Harry Beebee & Co.; that to the right by James Dobbie. Older premises existed here, but in 1910 both factories were rebuilt. Beebee's factory was demolished and the building shown was erected, constructed of red brick with sandstone dressings. The architect was Allan Stevenson, a noted Ayr architect of the time. In the same year the premises next door, owned by Dobbie, were rebuilt, the third floor being added to an older building. The louvres allowed the hides to dry, air being able to pass through the building. Again the architect for this extension was Stevenson. In later years both works were to come under the Beebee umbrella. In 1979 the business was taken over by the Bridge of Weir Leather Co. and the works closed down. Behind the tanneries can be seen the woollen mill of James Templeton & Son, also gone. The illustration was taken from a photograph taken in 1986, prior to the demolition of these buildings. The site has lain derelict since then, work only commencing in 2004 for the construction of a large shopping centre and associated parking.

AYR
OVERMILLS

The Over Mill at Ayr was one of the oldest mills on the river, having been founded as early as the thirteenth century, when it was operated by the monks, though one of the earliest known references to the mill dates from 1594. The buildings that latterly stood by the riverside, two miles east of the town centre, and adjacent to the present A77 by-pass, were naturally not so old as this, having been rebuilt numerous times over the centuries. One of the buildings was four storeys in height. What is known is that in 1761 a waulk mill was added for fulling, or beating, of cloth, and at this time the Over Mill became pluralized. In 1806 further improvements to the mill were made at a cost of £531. In later years the mill had a mill-wheel that was 20 feet in diameter by 5 feet across, capable of producing over 30 horsepower, and driving by means of shafts and gears five pairs of stones. The hoist was built in 1845, or thereabouts, made by J. & A. Taylor of Ayr. The mills had been the property of the Burgh of Ayr for over 300 years. The Over Mill was the last grain mill to remain in operation on the River Ayr, closing in 1959, and the buildings were demolished in the spring of 1963.

CATRINE MILL [I]

The original 'Big' or 'Old' mill at Catrine was erected in 1787 by Sir Claud Alexander, the local landowner, and David Dale, a noted industrialist who is better known for his connection with the mills at New Lanark. The mill stood in the centre of the village, in Mill Square, which is located two miles south east of Mauchline. Unfortunately, unlike the beautifully restored mills at New Lanark, Catrine's mill building was not to survive, and was closed in 1950. A firm from Saltcoats was commissioned to demolish the building, but whilst this was taking place the mill caught fire on 23 May 1963 and the demolition work was finished more quickly than expected. Dale proposed building the mill to Alexander in 1787 and within months work on it was under way. A Mr Abercrombie quoted £250 to build the mill, cut a lade and dam the River Ayr, but Dale reckoned this was too expensive and tried to reduce it. Whether or not Abercrombie designed the building or not is unknown. The mill rose five storeys in height, with an additional floor in the attic. The bulk of the structure was plain in style, but the central block, which projected considerably, was adorned with Venetian windows, arched lights and an imposing cupola, in which hung the cotton-works' bell. This had been cast in 1788 and weighed over 3 cwt, but in 1928 had to be recast, following a crack. At the roof corners of the main block were richly carved urns, a piece of elaborate ornamentation on what was basically a plain block. Inside, the main storeys were 10 feet in height, that in the attic being 7 feet 6 inches. The walls were up to 3 feet 6 inches thick in places, and under the roof were 25,636 square feet of workspace. The mill was lit by gaslight as early as 1814 – one of the many innovations employed there. In 1827 a pair of new waterwheels were added, 50 feet in diameter, producing a total of 480 horsepower. First turning on 31 March 1828, these wheels became a tourist attraction in their own right, with regular day trips from Glasgow to see them.

Top. Overmills, on the River Ayr.
Above. The original Catrine Mill building.

Top. The second Catrine Mill building.
Above. Pennyvenie Colliery at Dalmellington.

CATRINE MILL [II]

A massive investment in the mills at Catrine was undertaken in the post-war period, when a huge concrete and brick mill was erected between the River Ayr and the village's Mill Street. So large was the mill that the north side of the street was often left in shadow. The building was erected to plans drawn up by James Hay & Gabriel Steel, architects of Kilmarnock, and the work was carried out by the long-lasting local building firm, G. Reid & Son. Reginald Langford James, chairman of Finlay & Company, laid the foundation stone on 8 December 1945, and the new mill cost over £500,000 to construct. The main block was five storeys in height, and to the west of this was a long complex of three storeys. When it opened in 1950, it had the most up-to-date automated spinning and weaving machinery installed, hoping to keep Catrine at the forefront of the textile industry. There were 363 spinning looms in one shed. However, things were not to be, and the big mill was closed in 1968. At a later date Carrick Furniture Warehouse of Ayr, who advertised it as the largest furniture warehouse in Europe, used the building as a furniture store. However, that firm was later to close, and with it the depot in Catrine. The building was demolished and the site grassed over and trees planted on it, leaving an open space in the centre of the community, awaiting a future use. With the loss of two major industrial buildings right in the centre of the village, Catrine was to find itself out of the industrial race, and the remaining buildings lacked the bulk that made the village look other than a typical rural Ayrshire community.

DALMELLINGTON
PENNYVENIE MINE

Pennyvenie Colliery was established to the north east of Dalmellington, by the side of the Cumnock road, in 1881. The Dalmellington Iron Company operated the mine, which was to become known as 2, 3, 7 from the number of the shafts. Pennyvenie No. 2 was sunk in 1881 and produced its first coal in 1884. Shaft No. 3 was sunk at the same time, mining coal 39 fathoms below the ground. By October 1931 there were 288 men working below ground in the pit, and a further 56 on the surface. Shaft No. 7 was sunk in 1946 as part of a major redevelopment. This was 16 feet in diameter and 600 feet deep. Following this development the pit was able to produce around 1,000 tons of coal per day – twice its previous output. Shaft No. 3 was abandoned around 1960, leaving only shafts 2 and 7 in operation. In 1964 these two shafts employed 718 men. The miners worked the coal seams by the longwall method, there being 150 men employed here in 1977. The pit was closed in 1979 and the surface buildings demolished within the next two years. Only the bing, long noted for its burning centre, remains to mark where the pit once was.

KILBIRNIE
DENNYHOLM MILLS

Kilbirnie was noted for its various large mill complexes, which made cotton and other materials, but latterly specialised in the manufacture of nets. Most of these have closed down over the years, and in many cases have been converted for other uses. However, one that has gone is the Dennyholm Mill. This was erected around 1830 by William & James Knox as a flax spinning mill, mainly for the manufacture of thread. Over the years various rubble-built mill buildings were added or altered, and the two tall chimneys dominated the whole site. W. & J. Knox introduced steam power in 1855, the first in the town to do so. In later years, as the demand for threads made at Kilbirnie waned, Knox began to specialise in the manufacture of nets, and the mill was converted for this. The nearby Stoneyholm Mill, erected in 1831 to spin cotton, was taken over by Knox in 1864 and it too became a networks. Dennyholm mills were closed and most of the site cleared, but one range, four storeys in height, was converted into a sawmill. When this closed the buildings were left vacant for a number of years. Proposals to demolish them were hampered by the fact that the main building was listed. Always susceptible to vandalism, the mill was demolished in 1985 and the site redeveloped as the Dennyholm Wynd estate.

KILMARNOCK
BMK FACTORY

The BMK company was founded in Kilmarnock in 1908 with the merger of Robert Blackwood & Sons, carpet manufacturers, with Gavin Morton, textile manufacturers. The name of the company was officially Blackwood, Morton and Sons (Kilmarnock) Ltd., but this was soon abbreviated to BMK. Gavin Morton (1867–1954) had worked in his own family business, and invented a carpet power loom. However, the Mortons were unable to develop this, hence him joining William Blackwood to create the new company. The business was soon to develop quality carpets, which were in high demand all over the world.

Top. Dennyholm Mills at Kilbirnie.
Above. BMK carpet factory in Kilmarnock.

A massive factory was created at Burnside Street in the late 1920s, rising through eight floors and finished with large areas of plate glass windows. One side of this factory was curved to follow the line of the street, itself determined by the Kilmarnock Water, which flows past. On the roof, perched like an alien craft, was a large sign containing the famous initials. The massiveness of this factory was to become symbolic of Kilmarnock's industrial strength and technology. Demand for BMK carpets grew tremendously, and peaked before the Second World War, when they produced 5,000 carpets per week, in addition to 12,000 rugs and 20,000 yards of piece goods. BMK's reputation for quality meant that their carpets were specified for the best addresses in the world, and were laid on the floors of Hilton hotels, cruise ships, and airports. The demand for Kilmarnock-made carpets slumped in recent years, and the Burnside factory was closed in the early 1990s. The factory and many other industrial premises in the area were demolished and a supermarket and trading estate were erected on the site.

KILMARNOCK
LONGPARK POTTERY

In 1884 J. & M. Craig established a new works at Longpark, north of the town, for the manufacture of pottery items. This was located next to the Hillhead Fireclay Works which were noted for the manufacture of bricks, but which were closed and demolished prior to 1938. The Longpark Sanitary Pottery, as it became known, was taken over by the famous Shanks of Barrhead company in 1919. The works extended over quite an area between Hill Street and Hillhead Avenue and latterly were surrounded by housing. A small mineral

Longpark Pottery, Kilmarnock.

railway branch line entered the works from the west. The pottery had a number of large bottle kilns where produce such as wash-basins, toilet bowls and other bathroom ware was fired. These kilns had square brick bases and the towers were reinforced with steel bands. The upper courses of the kilns had alternate courses of red and white bricks, making them quite distinctive. At one time the works employed 300 people. There were two other sanitary-ware manufacturers in Kilmarnock, both of which have also gone. Southhook Potteries Ltd. was located at Bonnyton and made a variety of sinks, basins and glazed bricks, and J. & R. Howie's works was at Hurlford, established in 1854. Longpark pottery works were closed in 1981 and the whole site was cleared. It is now occupied by housing.

KILMARNOCK
ROWALLAN CREAMERY

John Wallace established a dairy company in 1886 and was to build a new creamery in what was a rural location to the north of Kilmarnock. This was opened on 28 August 1906. Known as the Rowallan Creamery, Wallace took in milk and used it to manufacture what was originally known as 'butterine'. In time this became known as margarine, and the Rowallan Creamery began to specialise in its manufacture. From 1923 only margarine was produced at the factory, and various products were developed. The company merged in 1953 with a Glasgow shortening manufacturer and new products were promoted

Rowallan Creamery, north of Kilmarnock.

Top. Saxone shoe factory, Kilmarnock.
Above. Mauchline Colliery.

around the country. In 1961 the business was taken over by Associated British Foods and margarine in tubs was promoted with considerable success. The creamery's better known brands, Banquet margarine and Sunflower margarine, became nationally recognised. The old sandstone factory was extended considerably, with the erection of a large red-brick building alongside, extending back some distance to take up much of the site, which occupied a promontory surrounded by the Fenwick Water. The creamery closed in 2002 and the buildings were subsequently demolished. Modern private housing was erected on the site.

KILMARNOCK
SAXONE SHOE FACTORY

Ayrshire has long had a history of shoe manufacture, and Saxone in Kilmarnock was one of the more successful. The company was founded in 1908 with the merger of Kilmarnock's Messrs Clark & Son (founded in 1820), later known as A.L. Clark & Co., with Abbott's of England. A new factory was erected between Titchfield Street and the Kilmarnock Water. This was a three-storey building with large areas of glazing, designed by the Kilmarnock architect Thomas Smellie. One of the main features of the building was the high water tower, on which the words Saxone Shoes were emblazoned, visible for miles around and echoed in the BMK sign on their Burnside Carpet Works, further south. A second Saxone factory was erected in Mill Street, known as the Gleneagles factory, in 1949 and a third, which specialised in repairs, was located in West Netherton Street. In 1956 Saxone merged with Lilley & Skinner and in 1962 became part of the British Shoe Corporation. The Titchfield Street factory was closed and demolished, the site being used for the Galleon leisure centre. The British Shoe Corporation decided to stop the manufacture of shoes, and sold the remaining Saxone properties to Burlington International in 1988, and in 1992 the Kilmarnock Shoe Company took over, making shoes at the Gleneagles factory.

MAUCHLINE COLLIERY

In 1925 Mauchline Colliery was sunk to the north of the village by Caprington and Auchlochan Collieries Ltd. The owner and director of the company lived in the village, at Beechgrove House. In 1934 this company went into liquidation and the pit was bought by Bairds and Dalmellington Co. Ltd. Bairds considerably extended the colliery. As part of the Coal Industry Social Welfare Organisation, which greatly enhanced the conditions experienced by the miners, pit-head baths were erected and they were opened on 6 July 1939 by R.L. Angus of Ladykirk. There were 42 showers, constructed at a cost of £13,148. At the same time as the baths were erected a new pit canteen was added, costing £800. Mauchline Colliery continued to employ many local men in the coalmine, and attracted others from as far away as Hurlford and Kilmarnock. In 1947, when taken over by the National Coal Board, the pit employed 632 miners plus another 182 surface workers. They produced 310,000 tons of coal that year. In 1951 the pit employed 800 men, yielding 250,000 tons of coal. The pit was closed in 1966, but the surface buildings were retained for a time for screening coal from other mines, such as Sorn mine, which itself closed in 1983. The complex at Mauchline was finally closed and the buildings demolished, leaving only the pit bing to indicate its whereabouts.

MAYBOLE
JACK'S IMPLEMENT WORKS

The manufacture of agricultural machinery was long established in Maybole. One of the more successful businessmen in this field was Alexander Jack, who was succeeded by John Marshall. Alexander Jack was born at Auchendrane

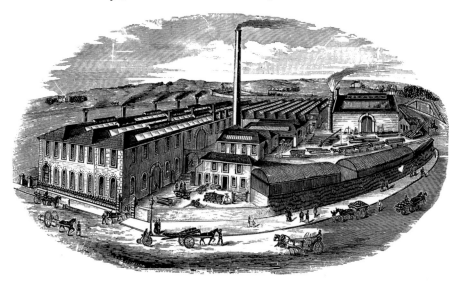

Maybole: Jack's Implement Works.

Mill, nearer to Ayr, and moved to Maybole in 1852. He started his business as the proud owner of one ten pound note, and began by manufacturing mason's mells. So successful was he that he diversified and started to make larger machinery, and soon was able to build the Townhead Works, located between Cassillis Road and Redbrae in Maybole, valued at £6,000. Alexander Jack died in 1877, but the business was kept going. In 1891 A. Jack & Sons, Ltd employed 1,000 people in the factory, producing a variety of implements for farmers, including reapers, carts and wagons. The works were extensive, including a number of major stone-built and slate-roofed buildings, and the tall chimney was a prominent local landmark. Jack's took over another Maybole implement maker, Thomas Hunter & Sons, whose factory was in Alloway Road. Hunter was noted for his ploughs and turnip sowers. In 1932 Jack's were the first company in Britain to make rubber-tyred carts. Jack's works were taken over by John Wallace after the Second World War, but with cheaper machinery produced elsewhere the works were closed in the early 1960s. Some of the buildings survive.

MAYBOLE
KIRKWYND FACTORY

The Kirkwynd factory in Maybole was one of the town's many boot and shoe factories, owned at one time by Charles Crawford. He, and John Gray, had the

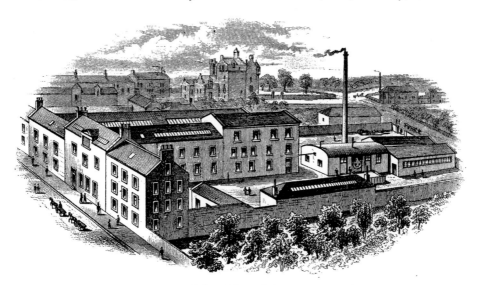

Maybole: Kirkwynd Factory.

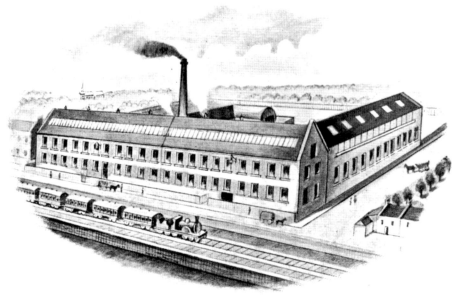

Top. Ladywell Tannery, Maybole.
Above. Townend Boot-and-Shoe Factory, Maybole.

distinction of noting that with the demise of weaving there would be a need for new industry in the town. Maybole had many notable springs, and Crawford and Gray realised that these were ideal to supply new tanneries, which in turn led to the manufacture of shoes. In 1891 there were ten footwear factories in the town, employing 1,500 workers. The Ladywell factory could account for 156 of these shoemakers, and was responsible for producing 2,000 pairs of shoes per week. Manufacture of shoes in Maybole really came to a close in 1968, when the last major factory, McCreath & Co., was closed down, leaving only a few very small specialist manufacturers. Maybole Castle is visible in the background of the illustration.

MAYBOLE
LADYWELL TANNERY

John Gray & Co. established the Ladywell Tannery and Shoe Factory in Maybole's Ladywell Road. The works were dominated by a tall three storey block, which had a fourth floor in the attic. Around this were numerous single-storey buildings and a large yard. In 1883 the factory employed 498 workers and produced 4,500 pairs of shoes every week, exported around the world, but mainly to Ireland. The factory closed in 1907. Being the largest in Maybole its closure brought considerable grief to the town, and many of its inhabitants emigrated at this time. After a spell of being idle, the factory was taken over by the Millar Tanning Co. Ltd and they started with only 45 workers. Business picked up and the number of employees increased. Latterly this was the only tanning business in Maybole. However, in May 1969 Millar's closed the business, laying off their last workers. The factory was demolished in the 1970s, the last part of it to be brought to the ground being the tall chimney, known locally as the 'Bog Lum'.

MAYBOLE
TOWNEND BOOT-AND-SHOE FACTORY

John Lees & Co. Ltd was one of Maybole's largest and longest-lasting boot and shoe manufacturers. The factory was established in 1878, next to the railway line, and in 1894 Lees took over the older Lorne Tannery. The main buildings formed an 'L' shape, the premises rising over two storeys and a third in the attic. Some of the building was notable for the large areas of glazing. Lees produced heavy boots for farm-workers, but demand for these fell with the introduction of the rubber Wellington boot. In 1928 the factory employed 350 workers. During the Second World War production was at full peak once more with the demand for boots for soldiers. However, when hostilities ended demand for locally-made shoes dwindled, and the factory gradually laid off its employees. Lees tried to introduce new machinery to cut the cost of production, but this was only to halt the decline temporarily. Despite diversifying into other commodities, Lees' business was brought to an end in June 1962 when the factory was destroyed by fire. The warehouses, located elsewhere in the town, were purchased by the local council and converted into a printworks.

MUIRKIRK GASWORKS

The gasworks in Muirkirk had the unique distinction of being the last town-gasworks in Britain still producing gas locally from coal. At one time there were hundreds, if not thousands, of similar works in communities all over the country, but gradually they were demolished either as larger works took over, or natural gas was piped in. The second last works in the country, at Biggar in Lanarkshire, were saved and remain preserved as an industrial museum, but the works at Muirkirk were demolished. With the opening of its gasworks in 1859 Muirkirk had the distinction of being the first village in Britain to be lit by gas. The works were located in Furnace Road, and appear in this illustration with the tall chimney, heavily strapped with iron. The main building is distinguished by its arched windows, and to the left of the chimney is the gasometer. Within the works was a horizontal retort. Muirkirk Coke and Gaslight Company operated the works initially. In 1977 North Sea Gas was piped into Muirkirk for the first time, and the old gasworks were closed.

MUIRKIRK IRONWORKS

In the second half of the eighteenth century the moors around Muirkirk were prospected for their mineral wealth. With generous quantities of coal and ironstone to be had, it was only a matter of time before entrepreneurs began hovering around the parish, and in 1785 Admiral Keith Stewart purchased the Wellwood estate. He and the Earl of Dundonald were instrumental in establishing major works in the area, including a tar kiln managed by John Loudon

Top. Muirkirk Gasworks.
Above. Muirkirk Ironworks.

MacAdam (1756–1836) of road-building fame, coal and ironstone mines and associated industries. Construction of the ironworks commenced in August 1787 and within a few years the furnaces were producing pig iron. They were owned by James Ewing & Co. and were the earliest to be established in Ayrshire. Mines were sunk to extract coal and ironstone, and around the old village new terraces of houses were built to house the vast influx of workers which increased the population by almost 500 per cent over a short period of time. The ironworks themselves were located on the south side of the village. The main furnace building had a most distinctive appearance, looking rather like a church tower, yet the locals knew it as 'The Castle'. This central tower had three floors of Gothic windows, each with hoodmoulds, and the parapet was crenellated. The rest of the ironworks were less attractive, being typical chimneys and sheds built of steel and brick. The ironworks were at their peak in the 1900s, but the local source of ironstone soon dried up, and the cost of importing stone was prohibitive. As a result the works were closed in 1923. Most were cleared away, but 'The Castle' remained in ruins for some time after this, eventually being taken down in 1968.

NEW CUMNOCK
BANK COLLIERY AND BRICKWORKS

There were a number of collieries with the Bank name, located to the south west of New Cumnock, near to Craigbank village. The pits were owned by the Hyslops of Bank House, and were latterly part of New Cumnock Collieries

New Cumnock: Bank Colliery and Brickworks.

Ltd. The accompanying illustration shows the New Bank Colliery (Pit No. 1), which was located to the south of Craigbank. The pit was sunk in the late 1800s and operated until 1969. Pit No. 2 of the colliery was located further to the east. On 17 October 1931 the new pithead baths were opened, established by the Miners' Welfare Committee, and available for miners to use, doing away with the need to bathe in tin baths at home. The photograph shows the pit buildings to the right, comprising steel-framed sheds with corrugated iron roofs. In 1946 there were 189 men working at the mine, producing around 115,000 tons of coal per annum. The pit horrals, or winding gear, is visible to the right of the chimney. The two chimneys to the left were associated with the Bank Brick Works, which were established next to the pit. The spoil from coal mines was often used for the manufacture of bricks, and a number of such works were set up throughout Ayrshire. Stamped with the word 'BANK' on them, the bricks were used far and wide for building purposes. Miners from the Bank pit established a reunion dinner once the pit was closed, and the 44th reunion was held in October 2003.

OCHILTREE
KILLOCH COLLIERY

The colliery established at North Killoch farm, to the west of the village of Ochiltree, was Ayrshire's largest and most prestigious coal mine ever. It was the most modern mine in the country at the time of its construction in 1953, and was the showpiece pit of the National Coal Board. The civil engineering and

Ochiltree: Killoch Colliery.

architectural firm of Egon Riss prepared the plans. The main features of the surface buildings were the two huge towers, constructed of steel and concrete, but with large areas of glazing overlooking the road. These rose 175 feet above the surrounding countryside and were prominent landmarks. Most buildings echoed these towers, concrete boxes with glazed fronts being the norm. The shafts were around 2,275 feet in depth, and it was planned to extract coal from the large Mauchline Basin reserves. The coal mine was dogged with difficulty from the time of its opening in 1960, mainly due to the abundance of faults in the coal seams. Indeed, it was claimed by local miners that the pit was erected on the wrong side of the road, and had it been built at South Killoch then it would have had a more successful life. Nevertheless, the mine was able to produce over 1,000,000 tons of coal per annum for many years, and in 1971 employed 2,165 men. The pit was closed in 1986 and the two large towers demolished a few years later. Some of the surface buildings were retained and converted into offices and workshops for a building firm.

PATNA
HOULDSWORTH COLLIERY

One of Bairds & Dalmellington Ltd's many coal mines, the shaft of Houldsworth Pit was started in 1899 and took two years to complete. The colliery was located high on the side of a moorland plateau to the north east of Patna, in Dalrymple parish. The surface buildings were situated just over 750 feet above sea level, and the shaft was 206 fathoms in depth, meaning that it mined coal seams in excess of 500 feet below sea level. At the time of sinking, the Houldsworth Pit was the deepest in Ayrshire, a record it held until 1909 when the Barony Pit at Auchinleck overtook it. The surface buildings of the pit were rather attractive, looking more like a Georgian orangery than a coal mine. The pit was named after the Houldsworth family, who had established the Dalmellington ironworks and who remained major shareholders in Bairds. In April 1907 an additional 140 men were taken on at the pit, and 40 workmen's houses were erected at Patna. In 1908 the pit employed 380 men, falling to 265 in 1946 and 224 in 1964. The output in 1947 was 81,000 tons. The pit was closed on 10 December 1965, by which time it was a property of the National Coal Board. However, it was subsequently reopened as a private mine. Renamed Smithston Mine, it was owned by T. Love, though in 1980 it employed only seven men underground and one on the surface. The depth-indicator from the winding engine is preserved in the North Ayrshire Museum at Saltcoats.

Patna: Houldsworth Colliery.

PRESTWICK
POW MILL

There were hundreds of small water-powered mills all over Ayrshire, each grinding corn, oats or for waulking cloth. Many of these buildings have been demolished, the need for them having long passed with the advent of mechanised farm machinery and the centralisation of manufactures. The Pow Mill in Prestwick was one of these, variously known as Powbank, or Powburn, and perhaps the original Prestwick Mill, mentioned in the thirteenth century. Located by the side of the Pow Burn, the mill ground corn for the local parish. It did not have much of a head of water, the slow-flowing Pow Burn being little more than a small stream. Nevertheless, it was dammed and the water released on demand to drive the wheel, which in turn worked the millstones. The main building was double-storey in height, the roof hipped at one end and with a jerkin head at the other. Here also was a tall chimney, added when the mill was converted to steam power. In the middle of the nineteenth century the miller was Hugh Ronald. The last miller was James Kennedy, who died in 1936. In later years the building was converted into a social club for men training to be pilots at Scottish Aviation's training school. The building was eventually demolished, and little remains to mark the site of the old dam.

Top. Pow Mill near Prestwick.
Above. Skeldon Mills on the River Doon.

SKELDON MILLS

The Skeldon mills, which stood on the north bank of the River Doon, two miles upstream from Dalrymple were also known in history as the Nethermill (according to Pont's map of 1654), or Nether Skeldon Mill. The mill was anciently a property of the Craufurds of Kerse and was little more than a meal mill. It had a breast paddle-wheel which could provide around 14 horsepower. However, some time in the first half of the nineteenth century the mill was rebuilt as a woollen mill. According to the *New Statistical Account*, written in 1837, the mill was at that time operated by William Templeton, who seems to have taken on the lease in 1800, 'a gentleman of great ingenuity and success, with respect to machinery. In the course of last year [i.e. 1836], Mr Templeton introduced gas light into his mill, which is of the greatest consequence and comfort to his workers.' By 1851 the tenant was David Templeton. In 1868 the mill was taken over by William T. Hammond, a nephew of James Templeton, carpet manufacturer in Ayr, and grandson of the Templetons of Skeldon. He specialised in the manufacture of what became known as Ayrshire or 'Skeldon Blankets', using wool from Ayrshire and Galloway sheep. As part of his improvements to the mill, he deepened and lengthened the tailrace by about half a mile, which allowed the head of water at the wheel to be increased to around nineteen feet. In 1890 the mill produced around 1,000 pairs of blankets per week, plus as much plaiding. Hammond sold the mills in 1894 to Miller & Porteous, who sold them on in 1917 to John Smith. In 1933 the Pickles family acquired them. In the 1940s a new turbine was installed, manufactured by Gilks of Kendal, which could produce 150 horsepower. Employment at the mill was around 100 in its hey-day, but before the Second World War this had dropped to 70. Thirty were employed in 1951, after which the mills were run down and closed. The mill-workers houses, which stood on the holm above the mill, were demolished between 1955 and 1964. Parts of the mill were later used for furniture manufacture and workshops.

SORN MINE

The Sorn Mine actually stood at East Montgarswood, half-way towards Mauchline. It was one of the last drift mines to be created in Ayrshire, having been established soon after 1947 by the National Coal Board. At that time the board was trying to modernise the industry in the county, closing the small ancient mines and developing new coal seams that previously had been too deep to work. The mine worked the coal of the Hurlford Main and MacNaught seams. Although one of the last mines to be sunk, it was one of the smaller collieries in the county, and did not have much of an architectural quality to it. In fact, there was little architectural pretence at all! Most of the buildings were either built of brick or steel girders and corrugated iron. The pit produced coal for many years, originally being sent to the larger Mauchline Colliery for screening, but when this closed it was redirected to Barony. In 1980 there were 246 miners working below ground at Sorn, and a further 18 were employed on the surface. The mine at Sorn was closed in 1983, and over the following years the surface buildings were removed, so that today there is little to be seen at East Montgarswood farm to indicate that it once existed.

STEVENSTON
ARDEER WORKS

In 1870 Alfred Nobel (1833–96), proprietor of the British Dynamite Company, or Nobel's Explosives Ltd, acquired the large area of rough ground, comprising sand dunes and salt flats, to the south east of Ardeer, and created a large explosives factory. Nobel was a Swedish chemist and had invented dynamite in 1867. The Swede, Alarik Liedbeck, designed most of the buildings within it but many later ones were by more local architects. The ornate double-storey building to the right of the illustration was the manager's house. Behind it, sporting a clock tower above the gable, was the office block. Built of bricks, it was decorated with contrasting bricks like a simpler version of Templeton's Carpet Factory on Glasgow Green. The office block was demolished in 1975. Beyond the main factory were hundreds of acres of blasting huts, surrounded by mounds of sand for safety reasons. At its peak, Nobel's, or ICI as it became in 1926, employed 12,700 workers and was to be the largest manufacturer of explosives in the world. Since the Second World War the number of employees at the factory has gradually diminished (5,000 workers in the 1970s; a few hundred today), and many of the buildings have been removed, as parts of the vast complex have been sold off. It wasn't just dynamite and nitro-glycerine that was made at Ardeer; there were later factories created to make polyesters, silicon and nylon, all of which have closed.

Top. Sorn Mine.
Above. The Nobel works at Ardeer, near Stevenston.

INDEX

Illustrations appearing in the book are highlighted in bold type